Elephant
Wars

Elephant Wars

◆

Why fight the Democrats when we have each other?

Get current commentary and more at
www.getelephantwars.com.

Gary Abernathy

iUniverse, Inc.
New York Lincoln Shanghai

Elephant Wars
Why fight the Democrats when we have each other?

Copyright © 2005 by Gary L. Abernathy

iUniverse books may be ordered through booksellers or by contacting:

iUniverse
2021 Pine Lake Road, Suite 100
Lincoln, NE 68512
www.iuniverse.com
1-800-Authors (1-800-288-4677)

ISBN-13: 978-0-595-35887-8 (pbk)
ISBN-13: 978-0-595-80343-9 (ebk)
ISBN-10: 0-595-35887-X (pbk)
ISBN-10: 0-595-80343-1 (ebk)

Printed in the United States of America

Contents

Author's note vii

Prologue 1

CHAPTER 1   Gary Abernathyfromohio meets the Warners. 5

CHAPTER 2   David starts swinging at Goliath 13

CHAPTER 3   New beginnings bring new dangers 19

CHAPTER 4   How much is it worth if it's free?. 28

CHAPTER 5   Kris Warner, hands-on Chairman 36

CHAPTER 6   Do what you want, as long as we approve 42

CHAPTER 7   One day is like a thousand years 48

CHAPTER 8   Bush whacked 57

CHAPTER 9   Can't we all just get along?. 66

CHAPTER 10   Trouble is our middle name 72

CHAPTER 11   Brother vs. Brother 80

CHAPTER 12   On the brink of disaster. 88

CHAPTER 13   Crunch time 95

CHAPTER 14   The State Republican Party versus Kris
             Warner 107

CHAPTER 15   Someone's gotta go, so I guess it'll be me. 113

CHAPTER 16   Do not go gentle into that good night 121

Epilogue 135

Author's note

I began writing this book early in 2003, when everything was looking up for the West Virginia Republican Party.

The results from the 2002 election gave us plenty of reason for optimism for the 2004 election cycle. I thought there was a good chance history could be made, in some fashion, and a chronicle of our achievements might be a worthy endeavor. At the time, I believed this book would be an account of how we turned West Virginia from a solidly Democrat state to at least one with a strong two-party system. And my boss, State Republican Chairman Kris Warner, was going to be the hero of the book.

As is often the case in life, fate had other plans. Indeed, we made some history in 2004, and reached some of our goals. But overall—because of our own inner-Party turmoil—we fell short of our objectives.

This book is a reflection of the events as they unfolded, becoming in the process a very different story than the one I set out to tell.

Prologue

As President George W. Bush took the stage—ahead of schedule, as usual—five thousand Mountaineers yelled, screamed and waved their banners in an outpouring of emotion and adulation that would have made Elvis proud.

In fact, Elvis himself had performed at this same Charleston, West Virginia, Civic Center more than 25 years earlier, as had every major act since 1959, from the Globetrotters to the Barnum & Bailey Circus to Snoop Dogg, but it was difficult to imagine any of them receiving a more tumultuous welcome than was being accorded the Leader of the Free World on this Halloween night in the fall of 2002.

After playing emcee and host for the pre-Presidential festivities, I was positioned with my wife, other State Party officials, candidates and guests at stage left on the massive platform that had been assembled in just 24 hours by a Civic Center crew working well into the night. Filling each wing of the giant stage were our Republican incumbents and challengers for the House of Delegates and State Senate, a coup pulled off through a series of begging, pleading and cajoling phone calls and emails to White House planners in the days leading up to the big event.

Seated on the rows of bleachers on center stage were Congresswoman Shelley Moore Capito, who was the primary beneficiary of the President's visit, and the requisite veterans (in uniform), Boy Scouts, minority faces, a state beauty queen and any other individual deemed politically correct and visually appealing enough to appear in camera range directly behind the President for the important images on the 11 o'clock news. A smattering of appreciative deep pocket donors completed the much sought after stage presence.

Allowing the cheers and applause to die slightly, the President surveyed the brightly colored signs and banners splattered throughout the crowd—most of which had been prepared the previous evening by volunteers instructed on exactly what wording to use. Finally, the Commander-in-Chief stepped to the podium, smiled, paused, and said with his sly Texas grin, "I'm glad I came," which, as he knew it would, sent the crowd into another prolonged frenzy.

George W. Bush was riding high. His poll numbers were near their zenith, bested only by the days and weeks immediately following the terrorist attacks of September 11, 2001. Last minute campaign swings like this one by the President on behalf of U.S. House and Senate candidates would result a few days later not only in the President's Party hanging on to the majority in Congress, but actually adding to it, a feat never before accomplished in any President's first midterm elections.

On that same Election Day—November 5, 2002—the Republican Party of West Virginia also managed to add 11 new members to the West Virginia Legislature, bringing our total numbers to 31 out of 100 in the House, 10 out of 34 in the Senate—a still dismal minority, but offering victory and justification enough to continue the course chartered when Kris Warner and I took over the reigns of the Party one year earlier.

In fact, there had been very little semblance of a State Republican Party to take over. Being a Republican in West Virginia was akin to being a fly in a restaurant—generally unwelcome, a distinct minority, and annoying at best. It was an analogy the state's Democrat Party Chairman was often fond of making in one fashion or another.

But State GOP Chairman Kris Warner and a handful of others fervently believed the politics of West Virginia were up for grabs. For sure, the state had elected an occasional Republican Governor from time to time. But the State Legislature had been firmly in the grasp of the Democrats for more than 70 straight years, and it was there the real power resided.

While West Virginia—the home of Senator-for-Life Robert C. Byrd, and the former Governor and longtime U.S. Senator Jay Rockefeller—was solidly rooted in Democrat history, it was also among the most socially conservative states in the Union. It had also consistently been among the poorest states in the nation, a long-held station in life that lent itself well to a simple political message of change.

Some cracks had already begun to appear in the Democrat armor. Bush won the state in a surprise upset in the 2000 election, the first non-incumbent Republican Presidential candidate to win West Virginia in decades. The reasons for the Bush victory in West Virginia were always a hot topic of debate, but it really boiled down to the fact that in West "By God" Virginia you did not dare threaten to take away the precious right to bear arms, or to get rid of coal in favor of some newfangled alternative energy source. Al Gore was seen as the leader of the pack on both those fronts, and, Democrat heritage or not, West Virginia was not about to elect Al Gore President.

That same year, Shelley Moore Capito was elected to Congress, the first Republican that West Virginia had sent to the U.S. House of Representatives in nearly 20 years. Capito was the daughter of former West Virginia Governor Arch

Moore, Jr., who, despite serving three years in jail for a variety of offenses, could probably, most West Virginians agreed, get elected again if he chose to run. Governor Moore had been credited with presiding over one of West Virginia's better economies and expanding its highway system, and crooked or not, he fit right in with the state's no-nonsense approach to life in general, i.e., the ends justify the means.

The one dark spot for Republicans in 2000 was the defeat of Governor Cecil Underwood, who holds the distinction of being both the youngest and oldest Governor in state history, having first been elected in 1954, then again in 1996. In 2000, former Congressman Bob Wise, whose open Congressional seat was the one picked off by Capito, narrowly defeated Underwood.

But gubernatorial races were not the bellwether of politics; they were more personality driven than reflective of Party or ideology. The real power resided in the gold-domed Statehouse in Charleston, with its 100 House of Delegates members and 34 State Senators. For the Republican Party of West Virginia, the Statehouse was the fortress that had to be attacked.

The main obstacle to battling the entrenched Democrats would not, in fact, be the Democrats. The main opposition would come from two Republican factions: GOP officeholders who had become so enslaved to the Democrat leadership that they had grown satisfied with whatever crumbs fell their way and had no interest in rocking the boat; and Republicans who, in the void left by the absence of a strong State Party, had started their own various clubs and auxiliaries and were not eager to surrender leadership or take direction from anyone else.

By registration, Democrats outnumbered Republicans in West Virginia 3 to 1—and as much as 8 to 1 in some regions of the state. The numbers themselves were discouraging to most Republicans who would even dream of making inroads. But many registered Democrats were Democrats in name only. Their philosophies, both socially and economically, were Republican to the core, and their registration was reflective more of a lack of Republican candidates on the ballot over the years than any allegiance to the Democrat Party.

It had taken thousands of Democrat crossover votes to elect both Bush and Capito, and many Republicans believed those voters could be "brought home" for good if there existed a strong, central State Republican Party organization headed by a leader with vision, conviction and commitment.

The night of October 31, 2002, gave those Republicans a small measure of satisfaction and a renewed sense of purpose. Our optimism was forgivable as we proudly surveyed the nearly 100 Republican candidates for state office we had managed to assemble on stage with the President of the United States. Two years ago, we knew, this would never have happened. The Bush team was typically too leery of offending Democrat voters in West Virginia with such a bold display of partisanship. But the fact they had agreed to allow the President to appear on stage this night surrounded by such a brazen Republican backdrop gave us a justifiable sense of progress.

I had been on the job in West Virginia for about a year by that time. When I took the job as Executive Director of the West Virginia Republican Party, I was as prepared as possible for the land mines we would encounter—but not nearly as prepared as I needed to be.

1

Gary Abernathyfromohio meets the Warners

In the fall of 2001, I was in my fourth year as Communications Director of the Ohio Republican Party, and I was clearly on cruise control. The Ohio GOP, with its staff of 25 full-time employees and already a powerhouse under the longtime leadership of Chairman Bob Bennett, was widely regarded as the best State Republican Party in the nation, challenged only, perhaps, by the GOP organizations in Florida and Texas.

When Bob Bennett became Ohio GOP Chairman in 1988, Democrats controlled everything—the statewide executive offices, the State Legislature, the Congressional delegation. Just eight short years later, the landscape had been completely reversed. And while Ohio's voter registration numbers had never been as lopsided as West Virginia's—Democrat and Republican voters split Ohio pretty evenly—the reversal of fortunes was no less impressive.

Bob Bennett was a large, loud Cleveland attorney with a northern "in-your-face" attitude. His temper tantrums toward his staff were the stuff of legend, and yet he engendered a loyalty and dedication from those same staffers that was difficult for outsiders to comprehend. Bennett would scream, yell, and sometimes literally throw things, but it would all take place behind closed doors, and he would never embarrass you publicly. In fact, to the public, Bennett would laud his staff as the best.

Bennett had been Chairman ten years when I joined the Ohio GOP. I was told that his personality had softened since a heart attack two years earlier, but if so, it was hard for me to imagine how this 60-year-old political boss could have been any fiercer than what I witnessed for myself. Still, I came to feel the same love and loyalty for him as others. He was a leader you wanted to please, not because you feared his wrath (at least, not *just* because you feared his wrath), but because he was loyal to you, and had surrounded you with the best and brightest

5

co-workers you could imagine. I was challenged on a daily basis to live up to the high quality surrounding me.

Until just a couple of years prior to joining the Ohio GOP, my career had been primarily as a newspaper editor, but I had suffered a severe case of journalism burnout, and my lifelong love of politics had landed me a job with an Ohio Congressman.

Late in 1997, I was informed by a couple of former fellow Congressional staff members of a job opening with the Ohio GOP. I was offered the job after an interview with Tom Whatman, the Executive Director of the Party, and I immediately made the move from Portsmouth, Ohio, to the capital city of Columbus.

Serving as Communications Director for the Ohio Republican Party came relatively easy to me. My background in newspapers had given me insight into how to deal with reporters whose main purpose was trying to dig dirt or find (or create) scandal. I was afforded two assistants who handled most of the technical aspects of the job (Web site development, recording studio production, graphic design for campaign literature), freeing me to concentrate on writing press releases, advertising scripts, speeches, developing special projects, handling the countless inquiries from the media, and serving as spokesman for the Party.

After four years and a national convention in Philadelphia in 2000, during which I sincerely believed I would die from exhaustion, I received a phone call from Whatman, who had moved on from the State Party to run his own independent consulting firm. Whatman, who knew I was interested in moving on as well, told me that the new Chairman of the West Virginia Republican Party, Kris Warner, was searching for an Executive Director.

Also involved in this mix was a young man named Collister "Coddy" Johnson. Coddy Johnson was in his mid 20s, and had been serving the Bush White House as a regional representative for a handful of states including both Ohio and West Virginia. Despite his youth, he was one of the smartest and most energetic individuals I had ever met in the political or business world.

After learning of my interest in the West Virginia job, Coddy called to enlighten me on some of the challenges I would face there from his point of view. In other words, he wanted to make sure I knew what I was getting myself into. Aside from the overwhelming political odds we were facing, Coddy spelled out the infighting and backbiting inherent in West Virginia politics.

Coddy, of course, had one objective above all others—making sure George W. Bush would win West Virginia again in 2004. He had little interest in Kris Warner's goal—Republican takeover of the State Legislature—but he did want a strong State Party in place to assist the Capito reelection campaign of 2002 and the Bush campaign in 2004, knowing firsthand how difficult the struggle had been for Bush forces in 2000 without an entrenched State Party organization.

I also sought the advice and wisdom of a political friend and Republican consultant named Jim Nathanson. Jim had served as Political Director at the Republican National Committee during the 1992 "Bush 41" campaign, and West Virginia had been one of his key states. He gently warned me that the internal Republican Party power struggles in the Mountain State had been among the worst he had ever witnessed, and urged me to think long and hard before stepping into that minefield.

Still, the challenges of West Virginia appealed to me immensely. I knew the odds were against us, but that was part of the appeal. In Ohio, we had reached the point where our job was to maintain the status quo—losing even one statewide executive race or any seat in the Legislature would be considered failure. In West Virginia, winning *anything* for the Republican side would be considered practically miraculous.

Plus, it was an opportunity to build a Party from scratch. By the time I had joined the Ohio staff, the State Party in the Buckeye State consisted of a full-time paid Chairman, an Executive Director, a Political Director with four field representatives, three full-time fundraisers, a three-person communications staff, two financial controllers (payroll, FEC reports, etc.) a Personnel Director, two secretaries, a full-time building maintenance and mailroom supervisor, and a plethora of other interns and part timers. The Party owned its own million dollar headquarters in Columbus, a massive, brick, three-story, white-columned complex the Democrats derisively described as the "Republican mansion on Rich Street."

I finally decided to call Kris Warner, who had just become acting Chairman of the West Virginia GOP, and after a brief discussion we scheduled a meeting in Charleston for the morning of September 12, 2001. After the chaos of the fateful events of September 11, I called Kris to ask if he still wanted to meet the following day. He said sure, why not? I soon came to understand that it would take more than a terrorist attack on the United States of America to dissuade Kris Warner from his goals—and as I would find out later, that was not always a good thing.

I will never forget the eerie early morning drive from Columbus to Charleston on September 12. It was still dark when I left Columbus, and the highways were practically deserted. I found myself watching the skies every mile of the way as dawn began to break. It's easy now to forget just how apprehensive the country was after those terrorist attacks, but that morning, none of us knew if more planes would fly into buildings, or if a nuclear device might be exploded somewhere.

Kris and I met at the local Bob Evans Restaurant that morning, and talked about philosophies, the condition of the Republican Party in West Virginia, and the kind of aggressive Party Kris was looking to build.

In West Virginia, I was joining a Party where the staff would consist of a volunteer Chairman, and a long serving woman named Donna Gosney (who was then wearing the Executive Director title). Our "headquarters" was a tiny three-room apartment near the State Capitol, and the Party struggled to make the $450 a month rent payment.

What the hell was I thinking?

The first challenge Warner had was trying to meet my salary needs. Aware of the West Virginia GOP's financial straits, I was willing to take the job for just slightly more money than I was currently making, but I could not afford to move for any less.

Kris Warner was taking over a Party that was $17,000 in debt, with no money on hand and no income on the horizon. Fundraising was nonexistent. But we agreed on my salary, and he promised to find a way to pay me. I took him at his word, and the deal was struck.

◆   ◆   ◆

Kris and I agreed that the first step for the new Republican Party in West Virginia was simply to make the state aware that we existed. One of his main reasons for asking me to take the job of Executive Director was my communications background, and it was understood from the beginning that I would be serving both roles. In fact, most of the time I would be filling every role possible.

While I was finishing up my duties in Ohio, Kris called one day to discuss setting up a press conference to announce my arrival.

"Who should we invite to be there with us?" he asked.

I thought about it for a moment. Knowing our legislative delegation was small and fractured, I thought it would be a bad idea to invite all of our Republican Legislators. If only a handful showed up, the press would focus not on who was there, but on who was absent.

"Who are our Republican leaders in the House and Senate?" I asked.

"Vic Sprouse in the Senate and Charles Trump in the House," Kris replied.

"Would they come?"

"Yeah, I think they would."

"Then let's invite them," I said. "They can represent all the other Republicans, and it will show support from our legislative leaders while at the same time avoiding the possible embarrassment of inviting all of our House and Senate members but having only a handful show up." Kris agreed, and Sprouse and Trump did indeed consent to be on hand.

The next step was to notify the press and try to drum up media interest in the West Virginia Republican Party bringing on a new Executive Director. To the West Virginia press, the Republican Party had long been a non-entity. And yet, generating interest among the press in West Virginia was not the huge challenge it might appear.

At the Ohio Party, we were covered regularly by several major news outlets, including *The Columbus Dispatch, The Cincinnati Enquirer, The Cincinnati Post, The* (Cleveland) *Plain Dealer*, the *Dayton Daily News*, the *Akron Beacon Journal*, the *Toledo Blade*, and the numerous TV and radio stations around the state. Each newspaper had a full time statehouse bureau reporter stationed in Columbus to cover politics and government.

In West Virginia, Charleston was the "major" city, the only one with a population exceeding 50,000. *The Charleston Gazette* was the state's most important newspaper. While there was also an afternoon Charleston paper, the *Charleston Daily Mail*, and daily newspapers in cities like Parkersburg, Wheeling, Huntington, Morgantown, Beckley and Martinsburg, they paled in comparison to the size and influence of the Ohio papers. The *Gazette* was the giant by West Virginia standards, and the goal was to get coverage in the *Gazette* and, hopefully, by the state's Associated Press bureau, which would hit all the other dailies.

The main political reporter for the notoriously leftwing *Gazette* was Fanny Seiler. As I soon came to learn, Fanny Seiler wielded enormous influence in politics and government in West Virginia, primarily through a thrice-weekly column on Sunday, Monday and Tuesday, when the *Gazette's* circulation soared over the rest of the week's editions. Fanny secured her power by writing a column filled with rumors and innuendo the likes of which few respectable newspapers in the country would allow. Politicians literally lived in fear of Fanny Seiler. They awakened early on the days her column appeared, hoping against hope to avoid seeing their names appear anywhere under her byline. Rumors of marital problems, drinking, gambling, or other personal issues were all fair game, with little evidence necessary other than her claim that she heard it from someone else.

Even before I hit the ground, Fanny had written about my impending arrival, making a point to report in each story that I was from Ohio and what my salary was going to be. Even though she was a little low on her estimate of my actual salary, it was an exorbitant enough figure to bring some early protests Kris' way from Republicans complaining about both the money and my out of state origins.

West Virginia has a lot of wonderful qualities. It is possibly the most physically beautiful state in the country. Its mountain terrain, dense forests and winding streams make for postcard vistas at almost every turn. Its people are honest, proud and hardworking—when they can find a job. They are also quite parochial. While they have a reputation for friendliness, a new resident soon realizes that you are either from West Virginia, born and raised, or you are forever an outsider. Democrat members of the Legislature questioned why Warner would bring someone from Ohio, with Senator Billy Wayne Bailey of Wyoming County offering constant criticism on that point in the coming months. Even many in the press reflected this attitude, and it became something of an inside joke each time the newspapers wrote about me and reported that I was "from Ohio." The punch line among my colleagues was that to the media, and many others, my name might as well be "Gary Abernathyfromohio."

At our initial press conference in November, 2001, which was as much a kick-off announcement for Kris as for me, the media turnout was good, including Fanny with the *Gazette*, a reporter from the *Daily Mail*, the Associated Press, and two TV stations. Fanny's first question to me was about my salary, and I deferred to Kris, who declined to discuss it, which only fueled the fires more.

A few short months later, Fanny tried to nail us on the Party's use of soft and hard fundraising dollars, stirring an issue that amounted to little more than a mild disagreement with the Secretary of State's office over the use of soft money transferred from the Republican National Committee. In the end, the question was resolved with a whimper instead of a bang (we were asked to transfer $10,000 from our Federal account back to our State account, which we agreed to do), but not before several alarmist headlines in the *Gazette* and a complete trashing on a local talk radio show.

By and large, as time went on, I was well received by most of my fellow Republicans in the Mountain State, and even Fanny Seiler and I warmed up to each other. Fanny was nearing the end of her career, which no one knew until she suddenly announced her retirement one day in early 2003. She had developed her own niche over a three-decade career with the *Gazette*, and I eventually learned what many politicians had learned over the years about Fanny: if you got to know her, and she you, you could develop a friendship and often use her column for your own ends. As time passed, I ended up being able to persuade Fanny to report some very favorable items about our efforts. Still, her style of rumor-based journalism was not something I missed when she finally put away her pen.

◆   ◆   ◆

Kris Warner was one of six brothers. I always teased him about being a member of the Ewing family, as in "Dallas," with all the brothers competing for the approval and favor of their daddy, George "Brud" Warner. Brud was a tall, distinguished looking gentleman who himself had served in the Legislature and other public offices. His sons were all overachievers, and the family had a strong tradition of military service, with the exception of Kris. I always felt Kris, then 40 and a married father of four (soon to be five) children, had within him an extra impetus to prove himself to the rest of his clan.

His oldest brother, Buffy, had served in the State Legislature, but then had broken the Warner mode by leaving West Virginia and opening a restaurant/bar on an island off the North Carolina coast, living the Jimmy Buffett experience. Next brother Kasey was a lawyer who had just been appointed United States Attorney for southern West Virginia. Then came Monty and Mac, both career military men, and Kris and Ben, who, along with Mac, went into business together in Morgantown, developing real estate. Their mother had passed away shortly before I arrived on the scene, and you could still see the hurt in all their faces over what was obviously a deeply heartfelt loss.

The Warners were not a wealthy family, but they had established themselves as a well known group of social and political activists. Kris, a longtime State Party Vice Chairman, was asked in the middle of 2001 to take the reigns of the state GOP, sought out for the job both by operatives in the Bush circle, as well as then-Chairman David Tyson.

Tyson was a Huntington attorney who was personable and smart, but many in the Party felt he was not committing the time or effort necessary to turn the Party around. Tyson and Kris were friends, and Kris, while sometimes moody and impatient, had built a reputation as a hard worker, impressing the Bush crowd with his efforts in the Morgantown region in recruiting volunteers and setting up phone banks in the waning days of the 2000 campaign.

Kasey, Monty and Mac were the three brothers Kris relied on most for political guidance and advice. I often found myself in a position of shooting down ideas from Kris that clearly had originated with one of his brothers. While they were all smart and somewhat experienced in politics, they were not familiar with the tactics that a State Party must pursue in order to be credible and to grow.

Their advice all too often was to go on the attack, and while state parties are certainly in a unique position to do so, and often should, there was a balancing act between knowing when and how to strike, and when to step back and let events play out on their own. For example, if the media was on the hunt against an opponent of ours, there was little to be gained from "piling on," and sometimes a lot to be lost.

Kris could only serve as acting Chairman until the full State Executive Committee met a few months later, but he didn't let the unofficial title hamper him. In addition to bringing me on board, we also lined up a Finance Director and a Political Director. Neither of the original people who took those jobs lasted too long, but that wasn't the point. Kris had clearly thrown down a gauntlet, gone out on a limb, both in regard to finances and reputation, and sent the message that his approach was serious, aggressive and long term.

To help erase the Party's debt, Kris approached a couple of friends and asked for a loan, which was the only means of meeting payroll the first several weeks of his new regime. Thankfully, the RNC agreed to send then-Chairman Jim Gilmore into Charleston for a fundraiser, which raised about $35,000, coupled with a check for $40,000 from the RNC itself to help us get started. Most of our contributions came from Republicans who had never before been involved in Party politics. Before the Gilmore event, a Charleston oil and gas man, James Reed, and his family came through for us prior to the Gilmore dinner with an initial contribution of $18,000, and without it I doubt we would have made it through the first month. With some money in the bank, debts paid, and his new team in place, the real work was about to begin.

2

David starts swinging at Goliath

There is an interesting dynamic that exists at state parties when your Party holds the White House. First, the Republican National Committee quickly becomes little more than a branch of the Bush campaign (just as the DNC had served President Clinton). Second, all 50 state Republican Parties are regarded as outposts of the RNC. The White House, RNC and, eventually, the Bush campaign could be very heavy handed in their effort to control and dictate the activities of each State Party. More than once, I had heard Bob Bennett in Ohio tell an RNC official on the phone to go to hell. The objectives of a State Party and a National Party are often at odds, with the State Party committed to Statehouse politics, the National Party only interested in the Presidency and the Congress.

Often on hand in Charleston during the 2002 campaign were three RNC regional representatives: political operative Randy Kammerdiener, communications representative Marcie Ridgeway, and finance representative Dorinda Moss, who would camp out at our tiny apartment office helping draw up get-out-the-vote (GOTV) plans and send fundraising appeals. The RNC's only real interest in West Virginia in 2002 was the reelection of Congresswoman Capito, but the side effects of its voter turnout program would help our entire ticket. The RNC spent thousands of dollars in voter turnout efforts that year, and it was obviously to our financial and political benefit to be as cooperative as possible.

The person we had brought on as our State Party fundraiser had quit early on for a higher paying and more secure job in his hometown of Huntington, leaving myself and Donna Gosney as the State Party's only two full-time paid employees. Donna had never completely warmed up to my arrival on the scene or Kris' direction for the Party. Donna was a nice lady and a dedicated Republican, but she was ill-equipped for our new demands. She continued to answer phones, help organize events and other light duties, but she never did fully commit to the new "team."

With Donna and me, and very often the three RNC people in town, our tiny office was sometimes a very uncomfortable place to be, with two people often sharing one desk. Kris, who spent most of his time in his Morgantown office, told me more than once that he didn't know how I did it, being cramped every day in those tiny rooms. In West Virginia, we were basically attempting to provide with just two employees and Kris Warner as many services to candidates and county Party chairmen as the Ohio Party typically provided with as many as 25 employees. I put in long, late night hours and weekends, but the excitement of what we were trying to achieve provided enough adrenalin to keep me energized.

When Randy, Marcie or Dorinda were in town from the RNC, they were often in our office cranking out mail, making phone calls and meeting with volunteers working on our GOTV program. Thanks to RNC money and our group of small but loyal donors, we were eventually able to rent the apartment across the hall for a couple of months leading up to the November 2002 election for volunteers to undertake a full scale GOTV effort.

Even though Kris Warner was officially my boss, the RNC had considerable influence on our finances and our success. The RNC had developed an amazing system of interaction with the state parties. Email, of course, played a huge role in communicating quickly and effectively, particularly on Federal issues. The media often contacted us for comments on the Capito race, and the RNC was upset if we strayed from their prepared talking points on Congressional races. There were some state parties, including Ohio, that were strong enough financially to ignore the RNC once in a while. In West Virginia, as I sometimes had to remind Kris Warner, we were still too dependent on the RNC's financial assistance to take that position (a fact of which the RNC was well aware) and more often than not we needed to salute and accept our marching orders.

Slowly, it appeared to me at the time, the Bush team began to share, on some level, our in-state belief that Republicans could win legislative races in West Virginia, and grew more willing to let us pursue that goal as long as it didn't hurt the Capito or Bush reelection efforts.

The relationship between the RNC and, eventually, the Bush campaign, on one hand, and the West Virginia Republican Party, on the other, continued to be a sometimes awkward and strained marriage of convenience. Most of the time, our goals were shared and mutually beneficial. Once in a while, we all had to agree to disagree and move on. But in 2001 and 2002, the Bush team held most of the cards, including the ability to help us financially by transferring money or sending in Cabinet secretaries and the like for the occasional State Party fundraiser.

In the long run, Kris and I adopted the philosophy that it was better to ask forgiveness than permission, and by and large we continued on our merry way, getting our hands slapped once in a while, but building a reputation for dedication, commitment and results, not only in the pursuit of our own goals but also on behalf of the Bush team as well. While they were not always completely happy with us, I felt the Bush team realized they were not likely to find anyone else to serve as Chairman or Executive Director in West Virginia who would be more committed to the cause. For several months, the Bush team and the State Party formed an alliance that was by and large productive and effective, and the occasional differences in objectives were largely smoothed over, or just ignored.

Certainly, finding people outside of West Virginia to relocate there was next to impossible—the state's (undeserved) reputation as a haven for hillbillies and rednecks, as well as its history as a seemingly impenetrable Democrat fortress, did not appeal to many of the most talented career GOP political operatives across the nation. Several of them did try locating in West Virginia to work, only to become quickly discouraged and leave on the first available plane.

With someday winning the State Legislature our main goal, Kris and I immediately went to work developing a plan to recruit Republican candidates for the state's House and Senate. Prior to the 2002 elections, we held only six of 34 Senate seats and 25 of 100 House seats. One of the main problems over the years in West Virginia was that Republicans simply would not run for office. They were either intimidated, or just believed it was impossible to win. So every election, countless Democrats walked back into office, uncontested.

Democrat officeholders were quick to denounce our efforts, of course. They claimed that recruiting candidates was a waste of time. "If you have to recruit someone, that means they don't have the fire in the belly and shouldn't be running anyway," was a familiar refrain. Another Democrat Legislator actually said in print, "Why would they run someone against me? I haven't done anything wrong." Some Democrats were so entrenched and so accustomed to being unchallenged, they truly did not understand any need for a two party system.

All of our GOP incumbents up for reelection in 2002 were committed to running and their seats were considered safe, in large part because of an attitude by the Democrats that as long as the Republicans were no serious threat, they would grant us a small minority of seats. Our focus, then, was on recruiting new candidates. Kris Warner put thousands of miles on his Lincoln Continental crisscrossing the state to follow up on any lead, meeting with countless individuals, trying to convince them to file candidacy papers. No one was off limits. Anyone willing to run with an "R" beside their name was sought out—school teachers, nurses, businessmen and women, retirees, veterans, even farmers—and promised the training, support and financial assistance of the Party, even as we had no idea where those finances would materialize.

Every two years, 117 candidates for the House and Senate run for the State Legislature in West Virginia—every House member (two-year terms) and half the State Senate (staggered four year terms). Our goal was to fill the ballot with 117 Republican candidates.

From my Ohio experience, I tried to bring as much training and services as possible, given the vast disparities in the personnel and technology that existed between the Ohio GOP and our meager beginnings in West Virginia. In early 2002, we scheduled an intensive two-day candidate training session at our head-quarters, devoting ourselves to one-on-one consultations with every new candidate. With Kris meeting with candidates in our outer office, and me in my cramped office one thin wall away, we jammed in more than 50 candidates for one-on-one sessions in less than 48 hours.

When the dust cleared from the Primary Election in May 2002, we were left with 84 Republican candidates for the 117 legislative races—short of our goal, but still more Republican candidates than at any time in recent West Virginia history.

While many of the "old guard" Republican incumbents were leery of our new approach (and some were downright hostile to us), our biggest allies were our new GOP challengers. By and large, they were excited about what we were trying to do, and shared our aggressive approach. Rank and file Republicans in West Virginia were tired of the attitude of resignation they felt had been adopted over the years by the State Republican Party and many of its officeholders. Whether we won or lost, they wanted a GOP that was at least competitive. Their encouragement, volunteerism and financial contributions sustained us that first year—even though we seldom had more than a month's operating funds on hand at any given time.

All during 2002, Kris and I worked tirelessly with our candidates, nearly forcing them to take part in training seminars and develop individual campaign plans. We managed to raise enough money to give the state maximum of $1,000 each to more than 40 candidates and a few County Party organizations for their GOTV efforts. By the time of President Bush's Charleston appearance on Halloween night, with our candidates lined up behind him on stage, Kris and I felt we had done just about everything we could do. It was in the hands of the voters now.

◆　　◆　　◆

There was a lot at stake on the Election Night of November 5, 2002. Many Republicans had warned us that our efforts to challenge so many Democrats might in fact hurt Congresswoman Capito's reelection effort against multi-millionaire trial lawyer Jim Humphreys, since a lot of Democrats had originally supported both Capito and Bush in 2000. If we failed to pick up seats, or if Capito lost, it would spell the end for Kris, me, and the new West Virginia Republican Party, which would not only cause joy among the Democrats, but among more than a few old-guard Republicans as well.

When the returns came in, though, Kris and I breathed a sigh of relief. Not only did Capito win by an amazing 20 points (compared to barely squeaking by against the same opponent in 2000), but Republicans picked up seven seats in the House of Delegates and four in the State Senate. Among our victories were upset wins over the Senate Judiciary Chairman (one of the best grassroots campaigns I ever saw by candidate Russ Weeks and his wife, Helen) and the Senate Finance Chairman.

The win over Democrat Oshel Craigo, the Senate Finance Chairman, was controversial. A bitter employee of Craigo's private business had contacted me one day with the news that Craigo was under Federal investigation. Kris told me he thought the information was legitimate, and we did a series of press releases on the subject, which became a big media story. Of course, the fact that Kris' brother, Kasey, was the U.S. Attorney whose office was doing the investigation brought howls of protest from the Democrats suggesting that Kasey was tipping off Kris for political purposes. I never witnessed any such communication between the brothers, but I also knew well who my Chairman's brother was. If Kris told me a tip seemed legitimate, I couldn't deny feeling safer about doing a press release on the subject. The investigation itself never did seem to yield any results, but the publicizing of it no doubt led to Craigo's defeat.

Almost all of our victorious House and Senate candidates were outspent by their opponents, but our candidates had worked harder, and, with our help, smarter. Later, in the spring of 2003, we also helped elect a Republican Mayor in Charleston, the capital city, another coup that added to our string of wins.

Not only had our victories justified our new approach, they also made believers among many of the Republican skeptics, who slowly began to come on board and get involved with our efforts. We had a fresh group of built-in loyalists among our newly-elected Republicans. The House and Senate leaders, Charles

Trump and Vic Sprouse, had largely been on our team from day one, much to their credit and our appreciation. Even Shelley Moore Capito had by and large been supportive, and her comfortable reelection victory only served to strengthen our bond. In fact, Capito and her staff would increasingly become allies with us in many battles to come with the Bush team, and her clout as the state's most important Republican officeholder could not be underestimated.

3

New beginnings bring new dangers

Throughout 2002, it appeared we had little choice but to continue to operate out of our cramped, dismal apartment offices along Kanawha Boulevard in Charleston. Even though West Virginia law prohibited corporate contributions, a Federal loophole did permit us to raise corporate money for the sole purpose of purchasing a headquarters. We had broached the subject occasionally with some potential corporate donors, but with the important election of November 2002 pending, we were not able to spend the time necessary to truly develop that kind of interest. Furthermore, the Federal loophole would come to an end with the enactment of Campaign Finance Reform, set to take effect the day after the 2002 elections.

But just three days before the election, Kris called me at the office.

"Hey," he said, in that urgent tone of voice I had come to recognize when he had some hot piece of information, "I think Don Blankenship is going to cut us a check for a hundred thousand."

I recognized the name Don Blankenship, Chairman and CEO of Massey Industries, the largest coal company in the state. Kris had been courting Blankenship heavily for contributions ever since becoming Chairman (the title had finally become official for Kris at the 2002 summer State Committee meeting).

"What?"

"Yeah, for a headquarters."

"How did this come about?" I asked.

"Just something I've been talking to him about."

"You know, we only have three days to do this before the law changes," I reminded him, unnecessarily.

"Listen," said Kris, "Blankenship's going to Fed Ex the check. I'm coming down this afternoon. See if you can set up meetings with Buck Harless and Jim Reed."

No further explanation was necessary. James "Buck" Harless was one of the largest political donors in the country. He had been the Bush Finance Chair in West Virginia in 2000, and gave a thousand dollars to the State Party from time to time—a pittance compared to what he gave to Bush and other political candidates of both parties. Jim Reed was our old friend who had originally helped us with startup costs. Harless spent most of his time in his southern West Virginia office, but by chance he was in town at his South Charleston office. He was able to meet with us late in the afternoon.

Technically, the purchase of a headquarters by a State Party is a major transaction that should receive the approval of the entire State Executive Committee. In West Virginia, our Committee consisted of about 140 individuals, a barely manageable group under the best of circumstances, and a nearly impossible obstacle under which to accomplish the quick purchase of a new headquarters. Kris and I decided to quickly appoint a 12-person Finance Committee made up of members of the full Committee, an option sanctioned under the bylaws, and we made calls to each member, explaining the circumstances and gaining their approval to proceed.

Meanwhile, I had called a real estate agent I knew through her occasional volunteer help, Teresa Cook, and asked her to arrange for Kris and me to take a look at any potential buildings in the area that might make a good headquarters. Kris and I met her at my office, and took a whirlwind tour of three or four potential sites.

"There's a place I want you guys to see in South Charleston," Teresa said after our second stop. South Charleston is not a reference to the southern end of Charleston. In fact, it is an incorporated city unto itself adjacent to Charleston. I knew that our Party bylaws, for some reason, stipulated that Party headquarters must be in Charleston, and I knew that if we bought a building outside the city of Charleston, there would be some Committee members who would grumble and make it an issue.

Nevertheless, the two-story building in South Charleston was ideal, with eight full offices, two conference rooms, a kitchen, two bathrooms, a basement for storage, and probably a partridge in a pear tree if we looked hard enough. It needed some cosmetic work, but otherwise would perfectly fit our needs. Ironically, a local steelworkers union, a group not typically friendly to Republicans, owned it.

The steelworkers' price was $250,000. Kris' knowledge of the real estate business came in handy, and he made an offer of $185,000, which was quickly accepted. In fact, the steelworkers offered to finance much of the purchase price themselves. They were in need of about $100,000 in quick cash in order to buy a new union hall for themselves, and securing that money was their main concern.

After touring the building, Kris and I rushed down the street to meet with Buck Harless, whose South Charleston office was ironically only a few blocks away. Buck's wife was sitting in the outer office, and she mentioned that she and Buck were getting ready to leave, waiting only for our meeting to be completed.

Buck stepped out and greeted us warmly. The stereotypical political big boss, Buck was an aging coal baron who usually had a cigar on his lips or a chew of tobacco inside his gums. Today the tobacco chaw was in favor. A large gold spittoon sat near his chair as we settled into his office, and he made frequent use of it.

Kris and I explained the reason for our visit, but I had the feeling we were not taking Buck by surprise. We mentioned that Don Blankenship was giving us a $100,000 corporate check toward the new headquarters. Later, I discovered that Buck was also a member of Blankenship's Massey Industries Board of Directors, and the two had few secrets between them.

Buck smiled, and said, "Don might be giving you a hundred thousand corporate, but he won't give you a hundred thousand personal money." He paused, and then added, "I'll give you $25,000 personal. I don't want to spend any company money on it."

Now, we were up to $125,000, and we thanked Buck sincerely but hurried off to meet with Jim Reed, who was also holding up his departure from his office in order to meet with us. Reed was a successful oil and gas developer, but not in a league with Massey Energy or Buck Harless. Still, he quickly agreed to contribute $10,000 in corporate funds. The next day, we secured $2,000 more from two other Charleston companies, bringing our grand total to $137,000. We set aside and pre-paid $17,000 for upgrades, meaning the steelworkers would finance $65,000, which, over a 10-year installment plan, cost us little more per month than we had been paying to rent two small apartments at our current location. Plus, for the first time in its history, the West Virginia Republican Party would own an asset worth roughly $200,000.

Under the law, the deal had to be closed by midnight on Election Day—papers signed, property transferred, and the money out of our hands. We consulted the RNC legal experts, whose opinion was that the money could be placed into trust, as long as it was out of our hands and out of our control. I called a local banker who, by coincidence, I had first befriended when we were both in Ohio, and he agreed to cut a certified check for the full amount while foregoing the normal three-day waiting period for our various checks to clear. Somehow we did it, but it's safe to say that few property transactions have started from scratch and been completed in the brief three-day window in which we accomplished the feat.

Knowing we would soon be relocating into an actual, honest to goodness headquarters had an immeasurably positive effect on my mental health heading into the New Year of 2003. However, I knew some other changes had to be made. The situation with Donna Gosney was simply not working out. Donna was a good-hearted person and probably tried her best to adjust, but she had spent too many years being a one-woman staff, basically operating for too long at her own leisure and whims to fully adjust to the new regime. She and Kris had always been at odds, and I wanted the move into the new headquarters to be a fresh start, and so I asked Donna for her resignation. It was a painful experience, for her and for me, but I felt it had to be done.

I called her into my office one day, and said, "Donna, I think we both know things are just not working out here, and I need to ask you to consider resigning."

Donna could not have been taken by too much surprise, but her eyes grew wide and she replied, "I really don't know what you're talking about."

I offered some explanations—discussing things I knew she already under-stood—and finally she said she would think about it, and returned to her desk. I felt badly. Donna was a nice woman, and a dedicated Republican, but the trust factor was not there, and she and Kris were oil and water.

Donna never did officially resign, but within a couple of weeks some sympa-thetic friends arranged for her to go to work at the Statehouse during the legisla-tive session, and she began slowly packing and removing her personal belongings day by day, until one day there was simply nothing else to take, and we said our goodbyes in as friendly a manner as we could under the circumstances. Donna had actually gotten elected to the State Executive Committee, so we both knew we had not seen the last of each other by a long shot.

Meanwhile, a bright young man and recent college graduate named Ben Beakes had joined our staff in late 2002 as our Political Director, and he helped carry a lot of the load. I also hired Olivia Kelley, another recent college graduate, to serve as our fundraiser. At our new headquarters, we were able to set aside office space for the Republican Women's Federation and the state Young Repub-lican organization, a gesture greatly appreciated by both groups and which helped build more goodwill among various GOP factions.

While the next big election of 2004 was nearly two years away, the planning by the Bush team was already in high gear. And for the 2004 legislative elections, we were once again in the business of recruiting enough candidates to completely fill the ballot for the 117 state legislative races—and this time, we were determined to meet that goal. But first, even with all the positive momentum, 2003 would prove to be a difficult year.

The McCain-Feingold Campaign Finance Reform (CFR) bill took effect the day after the 2002 General Election. It was a disastrous piece of legislation, especially for struggling state parties like the one in West Virginia. Previously, the RNC was able to transfer "soft" money to state parties to help with operating costs. CFR eliminated the national parties' ability to raise soft money (primarily corporate or union contributions, or money exceeding Federal limits), and the smaller state parties felt the crunch. In the previous two years, the RNC had given us $50,000 each year (the maximum our state law allowed them to give us in soft money), which went a long way toward getting us off to a good start.

Beginning the day after the 2002 elections, we started to struggle. After paying our bills from all the automated phone calls, literature and other vendor bills in which we had invested to help our candidates win, we were basically broke. While we were moving into a new headquarters—a move that would be completed by March 2003—we were immediately struggling to meet payroll, mortgage, insurance and utility payments. At one point in December of 2002, Kris had to ask his father for a $5,000 loan to the Party to help us to meet payroll. "Jock Ewing" came through, as did our friend and State Party treasurer, Brent Benjamin, with $3,000, but we struggled through almost all of 2003 trying desperately to raise enough money every week to keep the lights on and staff paid. West Virginia Republicans were still not accustomed to supporting a full-time, fully-staffed State Party organization, and in an "off year" like 2003, our appeals often fell on deaf ears.

Still, there were bright spots early in the New Year. The additional Republicans we added to the Legislature had an immediate and positive effect. After stalling for years on reforming issues such as Workers Compensation and tort reform, the Democrats in the Legislature, with an eye on the latest election results, decided they had better perform, and reforms, though not perfect, were passed on both those issues.

And Republican candidates for Governor in the 2004 election began coming out of the woodwork. Incumbent Democrat Governor Bob Wise, plagued by an extramarital scandal and some revolts from within his own Party, declared in mid-2003 he would not seek reelection. Two Democrats, Secretary of State Joe

Manchin and former State Sen. Lloyd Jackson, declared their candidacies, later joined by a third, attorney Jim Lees, and several lesser known candidates.

On the GOP side, Rob Capehart, a former State Tax and Revenue Secretary, had been running for about two years. He was soon joined by: Dr. Doug McKinney, a leader in the medical community; Larry Faircloth, a State Delegate from the Eastern Panhandle; State Senator Sarah Minear, who soon dropped out; millionaire former banker Dan Moore, who was no relation to the former Governor or Shelley Moore Capito, but whose last name and personal funds would do him no harm; South Charleston Mayor Richie Robb; and Monty Warner—yes, Kris Warner's brother, who had recently retired from a career in the U.S. Army. The Moore and Warner candidacies would both stir controversy within the Party, and the Warner campaign would turn out to be more disastrous than we could imagine. For now, though, Monty's entry in the race was merely a minor diversion.

Moore was widely known to be supported by his childhood friend and political kingmaker Buck Harless. Along with Harless' support came the assistance of Bill Phillips. In 2000, Phillips and Harless had served as the Bush Chair and Finance Chair respectively in West Virginia, and their open involvement with the Moore campaign brought immediate howls of protest from the other gubernatorial candidates who feared Moore would gain an immeasurable and unfair advantage if the Bush campaign was behind him.

The issue came to a head when First Lady Laura Bush was scheduled to come to Charleston in early October 2003 for a Bush-Cheney fundraiser. Invitations to the event prepared by Harless and Phillips listed several "honorary hosts," including Dan Moore, but no other gubernatorial candidate made the cut or apparently had even been invited to participate. Our phones soon began ringing with calls from Capehart, McKinney and Monty Warner expressing their anger. In turn, we referred them to Dave DenHerder, a Bush campaign regional political director who was responsible for a handful of states, including West Virginia.

I knew for a fact that on the national level, Karl Rove and company couldn't care less who won our Republican Primary for Governor, and the growing controversy—the Laura Bush incident had made its way into the press—could only spell trouble for the Bush campaign. Sure enough, DenHerder soon decided to pay a personal visit to the state, accompanied by his White House counterpart, Darren Bearson. The pair spent two days traveling the rugged terrain of the Mountain State and meeting with each major GOP candidate for Governor, assuring them the Bush campaign had no horse in this race.

DenHerder and Bearson seemed to understand that the Harless-Phillips connection with Moore could pose a major problem, but they had a difficult challenge trying to convince their bosses—Coddy Johnson (now the national campaign Field Director), Ken Mehlman (national Political Director) and Karl Rove (no title necessary)—of the seriousness of the issue. As far as Rove and Mehlman were concerned, Harless and Phillips were to be credited with Bush carrying West Virginia in 2000, against all odds. In fact, aside from Congresswoman Capito, Harless and Phillips were probably the only two West Virginians that Rove and Mehlman would recognize on sight. Believing that Harless was largely responsible for the Bush win in 2000 may not have been too much of a stretch. His fundraising and connections could be very persuasive in a small state like West Virginia.

Bill Phillips was a 60ish, thin, white-haired gentleman with a long history of behind-the-scenes political machinations in West Virginia. He had over time developed a distinct dislike—hatred was not too strong a word—for Kris Warner, for reasons that were never completely clear. His main complaint seemed to be that after helping Kris become State Chairman—a claim made by countless people—Kris had in turn failed to pay him the proper respect. As childish as this seemed, the egos in the political world would be beyond Sigmund Freud's comprehension, and Phillips refused to have any more dealings with Kris than absolutely necessary.

On the other hand, Phillips was fond of me. He praised my efforts at every opportunity. And I found Bill likeable on a personal level, although his attitude toward Kris and his ambivalence about the Republican Party in general left me shaking my head. I felt Bill had little interest in our efforts to elect Republicans on the statewide level, although he always insisted that he did. Phillips had a longstanding and close relationship with Harless, and he was quick to remind people of it. As 2003 progressed, though, Bill seemed to realize that his influence had lessened considerably, particular since the Bush folks wanted to stay out of the Governor's race, and Bill was diving in head first with the Dan Moore campaign. But as long as Johnson, Mehlman and Rove felt a loyalty to Phillips from his work in 2000, Bill would continue to be a player.

The Bush team, though, was increasingly willing to go around Phillips. In the wake of the Laura Bush invitation fiasco, the slow pace at which Phillips was building his Bush Steering Committee for 2004, his involvement as a consultant for Dan Moore, and the State Party's focus on in-state political success, the Bush team decided to bring in a full time Executive Director for the Bush campaign in West Virginia. The search began for someone outside the state (to avoid anyone here who had connections to one faction or the other), a development that could not have sat well with Bill Phillips.

Meanwhile, Monty Warner's candidacy for Governor brought its own head-aches. With Kris serving as State Chairman and brother Kasey as U.S. Attorney, there were many Republicans who felt the Monty Warner candidacy was just one more sign of an overt power grab on the part of the Warner brothers. It was clear to me that Monty's candidacy was fraught with peril for the stability of the Party, so on the night before Monty filed his exploratory papers, I asked Kris if he would mind if I met with Monty and personally expressed my concerns about his intentions. Kris said go for it.

I called Monty, and we arranged to meet in the parking lot of a nearby ele-mentary school. As dusk descended on the warm summer evening, Monty and I seated ourselves on a concrete barrier adjacent to the brick school building.

Monty Warner was an imposing, bear of a man whose lifetime in the military had left him with a stern countenance and direct manner. In his late 40s, married with teenage children, he was seldom accustomed to being challenged.

"What's on your mind?" he asked immediately.

OK, no small talk. Fine.

"I understand you're planning to file your exploratory papers tomorrow, and I'm not here to try to talk you out of that," I began. "But there are some concerns I need to share, or I'd feel like I wasn't doing my job."

He stared holes through me, but I trudged on. I said that with Kris being Party Chairman and Kasey being U.S. Attorney, a lot of Republicans would con-sider Monty's candidacy another sign of a blatant power grab by the Warners. I said that many Republicans would obviously believe, rightly or wrongly, that Kris would use the State Party to support him behind the scenes during the Primary campaign. I explained that many donors who were supporting one of the other GOP candidates could decide to punish the State Party by drying up our contri-butions. I said that in a worst case scenario, there might even be pressure from the State Executive Committee for Kris to resign. Monty sat staring straight into my eyes during my lengthy and one-way discourse.

"Are you finished?" he asked.

"Yep," I said, bracing myself for his response. I was glad I was braced. It was clear that Monty was barely containing his anger. His jaw was clenched and his eyes were red. I was frankly surprised at his anger. I had believed that Kris had probably tipped him off as to why I wanted to meet with him, but in fact, that did not seem to be the case. My words were clearly taking Monty by complete surprise.

In essence, Monty just could not understand the conflict. He was his own man, he declared. Just because his last name was Warner, why should that disqualify him from seeking office?

"Are you planning to have this conversation with the other candidates?" he demanded.

He was clearly hurt and offended. Monty always had a way of peppering almost any discussion with appeals to patriotism and references to history, and this night was no different. I countered here and there with rebuttals, but to no avail. Monty sincerely could not understand why anyone would consider it a conflict for the brother of the State Republican Chairman to seek the Republican nomination for Governor in a contested Primary.

After about an hour, Monty had calmed somewhat and eventually said he appreciated that I was doing my job in trying to look out for the best interests of my Chairman. He promised to consider what I had said, but it was clear there was no altering his course. We shook hands and went our separate ways.

The whole event helped clarify something for me about the Warner family, something that had always puzzled me in all my dealings with Kris. I had long been baffled by the fact that while Kris had a long and active history in politics, he could sometimes be surprisingly naïve about political realities. My own nature was that of a pragmatist—sometimes a pessimist—and it served me well in journalism and politics. Kris and Monty were not good at seeing the consequences of their actions. As one of our other statewide candidates once summed it up, they played checkers when they should have been playing chess.

I knew the Kris-Monty issue would rear its head at some point. At the time, though, I still held out hope it would be only a minor distraction and not the major controversy it would eventually become.

4

How much is it worth if it's free?

Filling the ballot with a complete slate of 117 Republican candidates for the State Legislature in the 2004 election seemed to be Kris Warner's burning passion above all else. He had been bitterly disappointed by falling short of that goal in 2002, a disappointment only somewhat lessened by our successes in the election.

To be sure, there were some parts of southern West Virginia where even finding a registered Republican was a challenge, let alone a registered Republican willing to put his or her name on the ballot. But Kris was determined, and made it clear to the staff that this challenge took precedent above all other issues.

Our point man for candidate recruitment was our Political Director, Ben Beakes. Ben had run in the 2002 GOP Primary for the House of Delegates in the 30th District, which was the Kanawha County/Charleston area where seven Delegates were to be elected. We actually had nine GOP candidates in the Primary for that race, and Ben, being young and unknown, did not make the cut. But his zeal and intelligence had impressed us, and he jumped at our offer to become our Political Director.

A lifelong West Virginian, Ben was familiar with the state and soon became an expert on each State Senate and Delegate district, developing an uncanny ability to immediately summon on demand the logistics of each district, who held what seat, and where we needed challengers. If anything, Ben was often a little too eager and excited about his job, and I sometimes had to draw him back, lest his enthusiasm lead him into making public comments with which we did not agree, or promises we could not keep.

Ben had to learn that once he was an employee of the Party, his every word could be taken as coming directly from the Chairman or from me, and we needed to maintain some level of control over what was being said on the Party's behalf.

But overall, Ben was a real find, and his youthful exuberance played well in front of our sometimes-jaded State Executive Committee, County Chairs, and other longtime politicos who could not help but be impressed by his pure optimism and dedication to the cause. Ben spent nearly every day of 2003 burning up the phone lines with County Chairmen and other grassroots activists, chasing down every lead or rumor about someone interested in running for the Legislature as a Republican.

Some days were discouraging indeed, as he was unable to persuade one potential candidate after another. Other days were more rewarding, with a commitment here or there. When we came across a particularly desirable candidate who was still on the fence, Kris himself would follow up with a personal plea from the Chairman. Still, the going was slow and the numbers were not adding up as quickly as we had hoped.

One day in mid November of 2003, Kris called me after speaking with one of our telephone vendors. He was considering purchasing a round of about 35,000 automated calls directed to the regions of the state where we still needed candidates, with a recording of him making a personal plea. The calls would be targeted toward registered Republicans, and the cost would be about $2,000.

At first, I was skeptical. A vendor had gotten directly through to Kris, and he was always a ready and willing audience for the pitch. But with the January filing deadline drawing closer, I did not try to talk Kris out of his latest brainstorm. I was doubtful, though, as to its chances for success.

Political telephone vendors have learned to do remarkable things with new technology. The kind of phone calls Kris had agreed to purchase involved supplying the vendor with our files of names and telephone numbers from those areas of the state where we still needed candidates. The automated system would dial each number. If a live person answered the call, they would be immediately disconnected. If the phone rang endlessly without a pickup, the call was disconnected as well. The targets of the calls were answering machines, so the calls were scheduled during the day when most people were at work or away from their homes for whatever reason. Only when an answering machine came on would the call kick in, and Kris Warner's voice would leave his prerecorded message, which went like this:

> *This is Kris Warner. Sorry I missed you. I'm calling because as Chairman of the West Virginia Republican Party, I need your help to find good Republican candidates for the House of Delegates and State Senate. I'm asking you to consider being a candidate for the House or Senate, or to let me know the name of someone who would make a great candidate. Please give me a call at 1-800...."*

Registered Republicans would return home in the evenings from their jobs and find what sounded like a very personal message from Kris Warner, asking for their help. It was a wonderful system, and was most often deployed for fundraising appeals or to invite people to attend a big rally where a large crowd was needed. I was anxious to see its effectiveness for candidate recruitment.

The 800 number Kris left on thousands of answering machines was the State Party's toll free number, and rang into our regular phone lines. To my amazement, people began calling at around 4 p.m., asking for Kris Warner, saying they were returning his call.

"Kris isn't in right now," I told the callers, just as Ben and Olivia were doing when they picked up the phone, "but I can help you. We're trying to find good Republican candidates for House and Senate races for next year's election. Is that something you might be interested in?" Of course they were, on some level anyway, or they wouldn't have been calling.

The calls kept coming—not tying up our four lines, necessarily, but coming in steadily and consistently, one every 10 or 15 minutes throughout the evening, as well as over the course of the next couple of days. All told, we received about 50 return calls from Kris' recorded plea for candidates. A couple of callers were Democrats upset about receiving the call (the system wasn't completely perfect) and one or two from individuals who just did not understand what the call was about. And, of course, we received a couple of calls from Republican incumbents who had learned of the calls and mistakenly believed we were trying to recruit candidates to run against them in the Primary. But the vast majority of calls were from people either interested in running for office themselves, or suggesting people they knew. Over the course of the next couple of weeks, we received 10 commitments to run for the State Legislature directly as a result of Kris' recorded phone calls, many in areas of the state where I doubt we could have found candidates any other way.

Despite the success of the automated calls, though, we still needed about 20 more candidates for House and Senate races. Ben continued his traditional efforts, and we hired another young man named Mike Ankron for two months to assist Ben. Mike would make most of the phone calls to County Chairs and potential candidates, while Ben spent more time on the road engaging in more direct arm twisting. Our numbers continued to grow as we saw ourselves inching closer to our goal.

◆   ◆   ◆

Aside from overseeing the staff, helping Kris with strategy, and keeping the peace between the Bush team and the State Party, my focus remained primarily on communicating our message. We had built a blast email list of several thousand names, allowing us to keep in frequent contact with grassroots Republicans all over the state. We helped teach candidates how to do press releases and trained them to stay on message. But above all else, my constant efforts were simply in trying to keep the West Virginia Republican Party in the public eye, through the media.

We were too poor most of the time to afford to buy any advertising, so we counted heavily on free, or "earned," media, as it's called in the business. One advantage we had was that for so many years the state had been dominated by one Party, and the press—even those with Democrat leanings—was grateful, at least for story purposes, that something had come along to counter the status quo. At first, we were ignored more often than not, but gradually we developed a relationship with most of the TV, radio and print reporters who covered politics in West Virginia. We issued at least one press release a week, sometimes two or three, and sometimes two or three in a single day. More and more, our press releases were being picked up and developed into full blown stories.

At one point the State Democrat Chairman complained in print that the Republican Party would say anything if we thought it would get us in the news. That, sir, would be correct.

If the Governor announced a new project, we immediately responded with what a lousy project it was. If a news story showed up talking about more layoffs or factory closings, we put out a press release blaming it on the Democrats, or the "Ruling Party," as we called them. The state was in such an economic mess it was easy to throw stones, and we threw them with glee. TV reporters increasingly sought us out for responses, and newspaper reporters learned there was always a story to be found here on a slow news day.

We sometimes scooped the Democrats on their own inner-party turmoil, a feat that probably drew more media attention than almost anything else we did. Through many political and business contacts around the state, we sometimes picked up word of impending moves by the Democrats.

I'll never forget the first time we did it. In early 2003, Kris learned that the current Democrat Chairman, Pat Maroney, was about to be replaced by state Division of Environmental Protection Director Mike Callaghan, who was much closer to Governor Wise. At this point, Wise was still planning to seek reelection, and apparently wanted his own handpicked person to run the State Democrat Party. Kris called me that evening to share the news, just so I would know.

"How sure are you?" I asked.

"Oh, this is solid," he said, telling me where he had heard it.

I thought for a moment, and then suggested, "Why don't we just put out a press release and announce it before they do?"

He laughed out loud. "Wouldn't that piss them off big time?"

"No doubt," I said. "Let's go for it."

The next morning, we issued a press release declaring that Pat Maroney was about to resign as Democrat Chairman, and Mike Callaghan would replace him. The press jumped all over it, and Maroney vehemently denied the story. For a day or two, I began to wonder how sound our information really was. On the other hand, we weren't a newspaper. If we were wrong, so what? The Republicans got it wrong, that's all. We couldn't afford to be wrong very often, of course, or the press would begin to just ignore us. But I figured we could survive one wrong "scoop."

Within the week, though, the prediction came true, and the press credited us with breaking the news and quizzed us endlessly about our sources.

Not long after, we learned that Governor Wise, caught up in a sex scandal with a subordinate, had sent an email to certain staff members letting them know he was not going to seek reelection. Once again, we beat everybody to the punch, announcing immediately that Wise had decided not to run again. Wise angrily denied the claim, and said he had made no such decision. But again, within days we were proven right, as Wise glumly announced he was stepping out of the race, although he claimed our "prediction" was just a "lucky guess."

By now, though, the press was doing stories on how the Republican Party of West Virginia was breaking news about Democrat activities. The Associated Press wrote a story on Aug. 11, 2003, headlined, "Aggressive GOP stirs state's political waters." AP reporter Gavin McCormick wrote, "They've come in dribs and drabs since January, a sporadic flow of press releases from Party headquarters announcing political plans of the state's Democrat bigwigs. The only surprise is that the announcements have come from the state Republican Party."

The story pointed out that Warner and the state GOP had succeeded in "creating storms" during a normally smooth off season, and quoted a longtime Democrat activist, Mike Plante, as saying Warner "has brought a lot of energy to the Party."

New Democrat Chairman Mike Callaghan was more defensive in the story, claiming that West Virginia Democrats were ready to meet the GOP challenge "head-on."

Meeting the Republicans head-on? The tiny, little, insignificant Republican Party? Television stories and radio talk show hosts picked up the same theme, much to our joy and surprise. From day one, I had been amazed that the Democrat Party in West Virginia even acknowledged us at all. That was their big mistake. If I had been advising the Democrats, I would have insisted that they never acknowledge the Republican Party's existence. But, thanks to their own lack of media savvy, the public recognition by the powerful West Virginia Democrat Party helped elevate the State GOP to a status of almost equal footing that would have otherwise taken years to earn through actual election victories.

Is it really any wonder we felt we could beat these guys? They had gone so many years with so little opposition, they simply were not prepared for battle. We were happy to have their help, and we continued to take advantage of every opportunity.

I had developed good relationships with most of the political reporters around West Virginia. As a former newspaper guy, I seldom saw the bias in the media that many Republicans felt was always there. Sure, most mainstream media reporters are more liberal than conservative, but most are also basically fair and more interested in a good story than the politics of those involved.

Hoppy Kercheval was an extremely influential West Virginian with a daily morning two-hour radio show, "Talkline," headquartered at WAJR in Morgantown, but broadcast on a network covering the entire state. Hoppy was smart, political, and a great reporter as well as talk show host, making a daily round of afternoon calls to sources far and wide, digging into the latest rumors or theories. A self-described political junkie, Hoppy was seen as personally leaning Republican, but not so much that the GOP was ever beyond his criticism. He was that rare interviewer who would treat his guests with respect, yet still probe effectively to get the answers he was seeking. And if he thought he was being stonewalled or misled, he said so without hesitation.

West Virginia had a variety of good, smart, and often caustic radio hosts. In addition to Hoppy, there were Rick Johnson and Stephen Reed (and later, Mike Agnello) at powerful WCHS in Charleston, Tom Roten at WVHU in Huntington, Jerry Waters at WVTS in Charleston, Jean Dean at WRVS in Huntington, and Steve O'Brien of WWNR in Beckley, just to name a few.

I also talked almost daily—on the record, off the record or on background—with newspaper reporters around the state, but primarily with *The Charleston Gazette's* Phil Kabler, Tom Searls, Scott Finn or Eric Eyre, the *Charleston Daily Mail's* Toby Coleman and Josh Hafenbrack, Mannix Porterfield of the *Beckley Register Herald*, and Lawrence Messina and Michelle Saxton of the state's Associated Press bureaus.

Local television reporters are usually the least politically knowledgeable members of the media. But there are exceptions, and Charleston had more than its share, including Scott Saxton of NBC affiliate WSAZ-TV (and husband of the AP's Michelle Saxton), Ben Thompson of WOWK-TV, the CBS station, and Kenny Bass of WCHS-TV, the ABC affiliate. They were usually on top of their game, and Saxton in particular was politically savvy.

It was highly unusual if a week went by without a media story referencing the State GOP. But as 2003 drew to a close and the big 2004 battle loomed before us. Kris and I agreed we needed some media attention with a little more meat to continue pushing our cause. We asked our Republican State House and Senate leaders, Charles Trump and Vic Sprouse, to meet with us and devise a Republican strategy for the upcoming legislative session in January.

Kris and I wanted our Republican officeholders to announce some bold initiatives for the January session, a session which normally would be little more than a caretaker assembly in a big election year. Through a long series of meetings, emails and rewrites, we came up with a document I somewhat pretentiously titled "The GOP Positive Bold Agenda for Growth." We held a press conference in the State Capitol Building, with Kris surrounded by Trump, Sprouse and the majority of our GOP caucus. The press turnout was great, with all major outlets in attendance.

Kris, in his prepared remarks, said the people of West Virginia could not afford to wait until the elections of 2004 for progress in the state. He announced that Republicans would be introducing legislation in January to privatize Workers Comp within one year, phase out the state's food tax, end the business franchise tax, bring about the nonpartisan election of judges to reform our courts, and redirect education dollars to students and classrooms "where they are needed most."

The Workers Comp issue had long been controversial, and over-taxed West Virginians seldom heard talk of tax cuts. The court system in the state notoriously favored organized labor and granted nearly every Workers Comp injury claim or medical malpractice lawsuit, and the state's teachers were threatening a revolt over salaries and classroom needs. In other words, every issue hit home, and the press ran with it.

In reality, of course, Republicans still held too few seats to do anything the Democrats did not want to address. But we considered our media blitz a no-lose proposition: if the Democrats adopted any part of our platform, we would claim victory and campaign on the need for more Republicans to accomplish even greater things; or, if they refused to address any of it, we would campaign against the "do-nothing" Democrats and on the need for more Republicans so these important issues could be tackled.

In addition to our "earned media" via the press conference, we also purchased about $2,000 worth of advertising on Hoppy Kercheval's morning talk show, which was the most popular talk radio program in the state, carried on about 20 different stations around West Virginia. For five days leading up to the January legislative session, our ad would run twice a day on Hoppy's show, spelling out the Republican agenda and challenging the Democrats to act on it.

"Call your Delegate or Senator, and tell them to support the Republican agenda," the ad would conclude. Naturally, we would do a press release announcing the ads, which would spread the message much further than the ad itself.

Our mission was to focus the public and the media on the failings of the Democrats and the existence of a legitimate alternative—an alternative we wanted them to remember come Election Day.

5

Kris Warner, hands-on Chairman

There's a joke among Executive Directors of state political parties that everything would run great if it wasn't for the Chairman getting in the way.

It is only a joke, of course, but there is occasionally fire behind the smoke. Ohio GOP Chairman Bob Bennett was a well-established powerhouse in Ohio by the time I joined that staff, and I developed my perceptions through my Ohio experience. As Communications Director, I was one of several department heads serving under our Executive Director, Tom Whatman. My marching orders came directly from Whatman, who was usually the only member of the staff to confer directly with Bennett. While Bennett was a well paid, full time State Chairman, he would only be in his top floor office about half the work week. He lived in Cleveland, but the Party provided him a home in Columbus, as well as a car. A staff member would usually drive him around the state for his various meetings, primarily with large donors. Bennett was definitely from the Ronald Reagan school of leadership: he set the tone, spelled out his objectives, and left it to Whatman and the staff to carry out the mission.

Only after more than a year on the job did I begin to meet semi-regularly with Bennett myself. This happened in part because Whatman, by that time, had been on the job more than eight years and, after learning he could trust me to handle the Chairman, was more than happy for me to do so and leave him out of the mix and with one less worry on his plate. Still, I never carried out any direction from Bennett without making sure Whatman was aware of what Bennett was asking. About half the time, Whatman would disagree with a Bennett idea, and for good reason. He would say to me, "Don't worry about it. I'll talk to Bob," after which the subject, whatever it was, would seldom come up again.

In time, I learned on my own which directives from Bennett I should really act on and which ones I should just ignore. Bennett was a man of moods himself, and if a phone call or something in the morning paper struck a nerve, he might call me into his office and demand a press release or a course of action that, in reality, was ill advised. So if I felt he was just in one of his moods, I had learned to let it slide a while to see if it was mentioned again. Usually, it was not, and the matter would be forgotten. Once in a while, Bennett would check back to see if I was following up, and, of course, I said I was, after which I would call Whatman to let him know what was happening. Then it became Whatman's chore to talk our Chairman down.

To some, this merry-go-round of avoidance might have given the appearance that Bob Bennett was being ill served or ignored by his staff. In fact, that was far from the case. We deeply admired Bennett and all he had accomplished. Most of the time, we felt we were protecting him from himself, and he knew that and appreciated it, joking with us openly about it from time to time.

One day during my last year on the job, Whatman and I were sitting in Bennett's office. He had called us in on some question or another, and was waiting on our reply. Bennett had a habit of doing several things at once—reading the newspaper, glancing at his messages, reading his email, even talking on the phone, while at the same time carrying on a conversation with his staff seated in front of his desk. Whatever Bennett's question had been, he was reading the paper and only half listening to Whatman's vague reply. Whatman was a master at offering an explanation which seemed to say something but in reality said nothing. Tom was in the middle of his non-answer when the whole scene just struck me as hilarious, and I started laughing quietly to myself. Apparently, I wasn't laughing quietly enough, and Bennett peeked up over the edge of his newspaper and asked, "What's so funny?"

I couldn't help myself, and said, very honestly, "Chairman, Tom is sitting here giving you the biggest bulls**t answer I ever heard to a question in my life." Whatman burst out laughing as well, since everyone in the room already knew how true it was.

"Yeah," said Bennett with a smile, turning back to his newspaper, "he does that a lot." To this day, Whatman still laughingly accuses me of throwing him under the train. And that was true, but I knew the train wasn't moving, and Tom wouldn't get hurt.

Kris Warner was no Bob Bennett, and I say that as a fact, not as an insult. They each had their leadership styles, and they were very, very different. Kris had his hand in everything. For a while, it was not a problem, since for a long time there were only two staff members and it made sense for us to communicate often, which we did, at least 20 times a day by phone, he in Morgantown, and me in Charleston.

But as our staff grew, I tried to maintain some semblance of order and, frankly, distance between Kris and our staff. Ideally, the Chairman should deal with the Executive Director, and the Executive Director with the staff, and vice versa. But as we brought on Ben and Olivia and the various other part timers and volunteers we employed from time to time, Kris soon fell into a habit of picking up the phone and calling them directly, giving orders and making requests. Sometimes—and this was the problem—his instructions would seem to contradict directives that I had just given. This put the staff in an awkward position. Both Kris and I were their bosses; whose instructions should they obey?

One day, Ben came into my office and was clearly upset. He said Kris had just called and given him a series of instructions, and many of them contradicted what I had asked of him just hours earlier. I told him I would deal with it, and when he left I picked up the phone and called Kris.

I had tremendous respect for Kris Warner, and even though my experience and media savvy were no doubt important, none of what we were accomplishing would have been happening if Kris wasn't raising money and giving so much time and attention to the cause. His devotion to changing West Virginia seemed like a personal mission, and as a volunteer Chairman, it was difficult to fault him for anything, and I always treaded gingerly when doing so.

But there were days he could be extremely moody and short tempered. Sometimes, an innocent email from me might be greeted with a returning message from him saying something like, "Get your head in the game," leaving me to shake my head and wonder what the hell brought that on. Or, he would say, "Spare me your sarcasm," when no sarcasm whatsoever was included, intended, or implied, by any stretch of the imagination. Other days, he was happy and on top of the world, joking and excited.

I was never sure which mood he might have wandered into, except that whatever tone was evidenced in the first phone call of the morning usually lasted throughout the day. On this day, he had seemed stressed and somewhat sullen, but I needed to address the issue. I called him and explained the problem.

"Kris, it's important that you and I communicate before you give orders to the staff," I said, adding it would be best if he would just contact me directly, and let me deal with the staff. He basically agreed, and for a while we operated in that manner.

After a while, though, Kris' hour by hour, day by day ideas and orders became a modus operandi that obviously was not going to change much. In essence, Kris was often acting not only as Chairman but as Executive Director as well. When the subject came up, he was quick to defer to me, and he told everyone he encountered that I was in charge of day to day operations. But clearly, the Chairman-Executive Director relationship in West Virginia was going to operate much differently than the Ohio setup.

I had a choice to make: I could either demand that Kris back off and let me handle the staff—a choice that ultimately would have led to my departure, either because I would have gotten so frustrated I would have quit, or Kris would have fired me—or I could do my best to adjust to Kris' personality and hands-on approach.

In a way, it was hard to fault Kris. He had begun building a true State Party in West Virginia almost purely through force of will. I believed his heart was in the right place even if his methods were not particularly productive. He was too personally invested to be expected to change much. In the end, we seemed to settle into a compromise that worked as well as possible. He made sure I was aware of what he wanted to do from week to week, talking to me in advance and allowing me to shoot down ideas as long as I carefully pointed out to him why I thought something was not necessarily a good plan.

But I eventually became less resistant to Kris dealing directly with the staff on many issues, because it was driving me crazy to address every small item he called about, and it was easier to let him deal directly with the staff. For their part, the members of the staff learned to let me know if Kris was suggesting anything questionable to them.

Another item that became an issue from time to time was our communications setup. I was utilizing a program that allowed us to send emails to thousands of grassroots Republicans all over the state. At first, since they were sent from my email account, they went out under my name. Kris soon asked that an account be set up under his name, so messages could go out from him sometimes. No problem.

However, when Kris' brother, Monty, joined the Primary race for Governor, it struck me as patently unfair that the State Party continued sending out thousands of mass emails coming from the Warner name. Clearly, this would fuel the speculation among other Republican candidates and their supporters that the State Party was favoring Monty and subliminally promoting him by overuse of the Warner name on mass emails. Frankly, I was never convinced that Kris did not have the same idea, although I never raised it with him. Eventually, I set up an account that had all emails coming from "WVGOP."

The same issue came up in regard to media relations. Charleston was the hub of the media in West Virginia. Kris spent most of his time in Morgantown. When the Charleston media wanted a quick comment on one issue or the other, they generally contacted me, and the TV stations would often swing by our headquarters for a quick sound bite or interview. If Kris happened to be there, I was always happy to defer to him and set him up for the interviews. But if not, I handled it myself.

Once in a while, though, Kris would ask me to make sure that he did as many of the interviews as possible. He even pointed out that our CBS affiliate in Charleston was part of a statewide network, and he could go to the Morgantown affiliate and do an interview with them by satellite hookup. I knew this was something the Charleston station would seldom want to bother with, due to time restraints, especially if they just wanted a quick, 10-second response to something.

In Ohio, this had never been an issue. As Communications Director, it was my job to talk with the media. The only time we ever arranged for interviews with Bob Bennett was when the media was seeking a lengthier, in-depth story on one subject or another. And Bennett's ego was mature enough not to be threatened by the fact that his Communications Director was doing his job.

Kris Warner would often lecture people on the need to create a Republican Party in West Virginia that was about policies, not personalities. He believed, correctly, that the State GOP had too often been co-opted by either Arch Moore or Cecil Underwood when they had held the Governor's office, and turned it into the Moore Party or the Underwood Party. It was an admirable argument, but clearly Kris was himself sensitive to whose name and face were associated with the West Virginia GOP, and he wanted it to be his as much as possible.

I did not disagree in principle. The Chairman is, overall, the face of the Party. But one of the main reasons Kris specifically wanted me as his Executive Director was my communications experience. There were a lot of things Kris and others were more talented at than I was, but frankly, I was more experienced with TV or radio interviews than he was—particularly when it came to injecting some humor and staying on message—and he knew it, and his no-holds-barred comments often got us into hot water. If the goal was to communicate our message and promote our agenda, I was the most effective at doing it. Plus, I made sure in all my interviews to mention Kris' name and talk about the Party in terms of what it was accomplishing under his direction. But still, he was human. Taken alone, it was a relatively minor issue, but one that kept resurfacing often enough to develop the potential of a real problem.

No matter how well things were going for us at any given time, Kris could still find time to nitpick. He would send emails to the staff critiquing their spelling errors in inner-office emails (something almost no one worries about these days), or write our receptionist, Stephanie Snodgrass—who was very experienced in business before joining the Party—with detailed instructions on how to take messages.

From time to time I would raise the subject with Kris, gently suggesting he had more important things to worry about. But it was a perfect example of the type of thing Kris could get focused on until he was reminded that being Chairman of the West Virginia Republican Party carried more pressing duties than micromanaging our receptionist.

Overall, despite his moods and his controlling nature, I continued to think of Kris Warner as a good and generous man. His energy and drive always amazed me. He seldom slept more than four or five hours a night. He would ask for the moon when dealing with everyone from donors to the Bush team. Sometimes I cringed at the favors he would ask me to seek from the Bush folks, knowing there was not a chance in the world of having the request granted. But he operated from the premise that if you don't ask, you can't get it. And once in a blue moon his dreams would actually come true.

He was generous to a fault. Knowing how much my 12-year-old son loved to hunt, he went out of his way to set aside a Saturday—a day that was one of the coldest and snowiest of the year—to take us deer hunting on the Warner family farm.

Kris spent hours that day giving my son pointers, showing him the best place to wait quietly for deer, even providing a better rifle and hunting gear than we had brought with us. No one bagged a deer that day, but Kris' efforts meant a lot to my son, and to me.

He seldom argued about time off for the staff, and was always understanding about family obligations. Overall, I sincerely liked him, and whenever various issues came up that made me feel like walking away, I reminded myself of all his good qualities, his sincerity of purpose, and the prize that awaited us if we just stayed the course and made it to the finish line.

6

Do what you want, as long as we approve

Supporters of President Bush in West Virginia firmly believed the Mountain State was responsible for the Bush presidency in 2000. Part of this impression stemmed from the state's exceptional sense of pride and parochial notions. Certainly, George W. Bush would not have won the White House if West Virginia had voted for Al Gore. But the same could be said for every other state that went for Bush, including, obviously, Florida, or Gore's home state of Tennessee.

Still, West Virginia took full credit and believed that its five Electoral votes put Bush over the top. And winning the state was indeed an unexpected prize for the Bush campaign. Further, the Bush team was not about to let the state slip away in 2004.

The Bush team focused unprecedented money and manpower on the state of West Virginia for the 2004 election cycle. In addition to the regional field reps from the Bush campaign, the White House and the RNC who paid close, daily attention to West Virginia, the RNC paid the salary for a full time communications coordinator for the state, as well as a full time get-out-the-vote director, both of whom worked out of our headquarters. The communications person, Mary Diamond, was a former employee of Congresswoman Capito's, and her job was basically to make sure the President's message and agenda were being echoed in West Virginia's media. The original GOTV director was a young man named Ward Baker, who, in 2003 had been instrumental in electing Haley Barbour Governor of Mississippi through an unprecedented effort to get Republicans and other Barbour-leaning voters to the polls. Baker's efforts in particular would be good not only for President Bush and Shelley Moore Capito, but also for our GOP legislative candidates through its trickle-down effect.

But along with the assistance these people would provide also came the heavy hand of the Bush team. It cannot be stressed enough that the only mission of the

Bush team was to reelect President Bush. The Bush folks often stressed that the President did not want his reelection to be a "lonely victory." He wanted to have coattails, and he wanted to celebrate election night 2004 with a slew of new Republican officeholders, we were told.

But in reality, anything that might in the smallest way conflict with the Bush campaign plan or message was severely scrutinized and often squashed completely. In West Virginia, the Bush team had bought into the notion that a sizeable coalition of "non-traditional" Bush supporters was responsible for the victory in the state in 2000. "Non-traditional" was code for "Democrats." Therefore, the Bush team was constantly on guard for anything coming from the Republican side in West Virginia that seemed unduly harsh against Democrats. Between the RNC and the Bush campaign, there had emerged a "control team," dedicated to directing the activities and message of every Republican at the state, county and sometimes even precinct level.

Obviously, this philosophy was often at odds with the State Party's agenda, which was based on electing more Republican State Legislators and defeating as many Democrats as possible. Part of convincing voters to elect someone new is giving them a good reason to "fire" the incumbent. It was necessary for us to go on the attack from time to time. We never hesitated to rip into the Democrat leadership in the state, as well as the leading contenders for the Democrat gubernatorial nomination, Joe Manchin and Lloyd Jackson.

One attack in particular—against Jackson—brought the wrath of the Bush team. We had issued a press release shortly after Governor Wise announced he was not going to seek reelection. We said the Democrat "vultures" were already circling the body, referring to Jackson's announced intention to get into the race once his friend Bob Wise dropped out. We said that Jackson was the choice of "big labor bosses" meeting in "smoke-filled back rooms."

Such a pronouncement was pretty standard procedure for a state political party. Everyone understands that part of the job of a State Party is to attack the opposition in a way that a candidate himself often does not want to do. But shortly after issuing the release, I received a call from Coddy Johnson, now the national Field Coordinator with the Bush campaign.

"Gary, explain to me the purpose of that press release," Coddy demanded.

"Well," I said, searching for the words to describe what seemed to me a self-explanatory press release, "we're just trying to increase Lloyd Jackson's negatives. The unions will jump on board Jackson's campaign pretty soon, and we just want to plant the seed that the Democrat nominees are chosen by the union bosses and forced on the people."

"But Gary," said Coddy, "you have to keep in mind that the President is trying to set a new tone, and this kind of language is not what the President wants. Remember that we need a lot of Democrat votes, and the President had the support of a lot of Democrats in 2000. What the State Party says reflects on the President as well."

"I understand that," I replied, "and that's why we're always careful to attack the big labor bosses and the Democrat leadership, not rank and file Democrats."

But it wasn't long before the Bush team got serious about sending in its own communications person, Mary Diamond, to work out of our headquarters and try to control our messages and press releases. Mary was less concerned about the issues between the State Party and the Bush team than she was about the opportunity to expand her political experience. Working for Shelley Moore Capito's Congressional office, her talents had been largely wasted on routine press releases announcing government grants or highway projects. A former Bush campaign worker from 2000, Mary was anxious to get back into the action and excitement of a political campaign.

Kris and I, though, were ready to draw the line. While in 2002 we had been largely dependent on RNC money to continue our existence, those funds had dried up in 2003, due largely to Campaign Finance Reform (thousands of dollars were still being transferred to us from the RNC, but solely for the building of GOTV activities). We were surviving and operating now solely on our own fundraising efforts, and were much less amenable to the heavy hand of the RNC or the Bush campaign. We told Randy Kammerdiener and Dave DenHerder that Mary Diamond was welcome to work out of our headquarters, but we were not about to surrender our right to pursue our own agenda and adhere to our own plan to attack the Democrats, when necessary. We still wanted to be team players, but not at the cost of our own additional objectives.

In time, we reached another uneasy accord with the Bush team. We made it clear to Mary when she arrived that we planned to continue writing and issuing our own press releases. She was free to concentrate on the Bush message, and do whatever she needed in that regard, and Kris was happy to lend his name as State Chairman on whatever Bush message Mary developed. But we also made it clear that we would welcome no interference in regard to the State Party's message on state issues or candidates. To her credit, Mary seldom tried to interfere, and in fact over time became another ally with us in many of our struggles.

◆   ◆   ◆

The Republican Party of West Virginia needed to raise about $350,000 a year to meet operating costs and provide candidate support—a drop in the bucket to many state parties. About half of that was raised each year through an ongoing mail program—the $10, $25, $50 and $100 contributions are the lifeblood of every State Party. The other half of our budget came from large donor events.

While the RNC soft money flow came to an abrupt halt in 2003, the National Party did continue to help us by sending Bush "surrogates" into West Virginia for State Party fundraisers. In 2003, the West Virginia Republican Party was the beneficiary of fundraising visits from Health and Human Services Secretary Tommy Thompson, Commerce Secretary Don Evans, Energy Secretary Spencer Abraham, and former President and First Lady George and Barbara Bush.

By far, the most popular and lucrative visit was by the Bushes. The current President's father remained immensely popular among Republicans, but his drawing power might well be surpassed by his wife. Barbara Bush's reputation for telling it like it is, and her down-to-earth, comfortable style makes her a real favorite. The Bushes were, in fact, scheduled to be in state anyway for a private gig at the famous Greenbrier resort, on behalf of an insurance industry group. But the RNC asked them to appear at a State Party fundraiser, as long as we also held it at the Greenbrier. Originally, the Bush fundraiser was meant to benefit both Congresswoman Capito and the State Party. But Shelley Capito had just recently hosted Vice President Cheney for a fundraiser, and she felt she might be a little hard pressed to come right back at those same donors for another event with so little turnaround time. Plus, she knew the State Party was in need of the money, and agreed to let us have the whole event.

We charged $1,000 apiece for the Bush event, and raised $35,000. The former President and First Lady were both gracious with their time. They mingled with the guests and posed for photographs. Barbara brought along one of her new dogs, and it almost stole the show.

In West Virginia, anyone less than a current or former President was a difficult sell, a lesson the Bush team found hard to fathom. In most other states, a Cabinet official was good for $50,000 to $100,000 for a single fundraiser. Not in West Virginia, where fundraising laws were restrictive, people were just not easily impressed, and Republicans with money were scarce. We managed to raise about $12,000 each with the Thompson, Evans and Abraham events—good money for us, but well below what visits like these would have meant to other states.

In fact, Abraham—who had already cancelled on us twice—nearly canceled again the night before his scheduled visit when he learned how relatively little interest there was in his appearance. But some late arm twisting convinced him to follow through, since this time the State Party had already gone as far as paying for his plane ticket and the costs associated with the event site.

Early on, the Bush team was under the impression that the State Party simply wasn't doing a good job of trying to raise money. But after Dorinda Moss, the RNC fundraising field rep, spent a full week on the ground trying to raise money for one of the Cabinet level events, she reported back that West Virginia was the most difficult state in which she had ever tried to raise money.

The press always roundly criticizes fundraising events, especially ones involving a President, Vice President or Cabinet official. The media loves to insinuate that money buys access, and they always point to these fundraisers as proof positive. That was certainly true to some degree—a large contribution could indeed buy you a seat at the table with a Tommy Thompson or a Spencer Abraham. But the impression is that deals are being cut, policy is being developed, or state secrets are being shared. That's ridiculous.

Donors who buy their way into small, private roundtable events are rewarded with the same, drab policy statements that the guest of honor would make in any public setting. The donors usually do get to ask questions, but again, the answers are careful and noncommittal—nothing you wouldn't hear from the same official in a press conference setting. In reality, the most valuable thing a donor comes away with from these visits is a "grip'n'grin" handshake photograph in front of the American flag.

The idea that big contributors buy influence is one of the most exaggerated notions in the media, and among many in the general public. I won't argue that money talks, whether in politics, business or any other walk of life. But most contributors do not give because they want something in return. Rather, they give to the Party and candidate who already best reflect the philosophy of government in which they believe. In fact, my experience has been that the biggest arm twisters are donors who really don't give all that much money.

In West Virginia, the largest contribution we could accept from any one individual was $11,000—$10,000 into our Federal account, $1,000 into our State account. We had a handful of donors at that level, and few of them ever asked for anything in return, other than to elect more Republicans. But there were other individuals who, because of their annual donation of $500 or maybe $1,000, felt they had bought the Party lock, stock and barrel, and never in any conversation failed to remind us of their generosity.

Just like in business, political parties have to deal with deadbeats. Many times, people would reserve a spot for themselves at an event and promise to get the check to us "next week," which is apparently code for "never." We had to eventually adopt a strict policy of payment up front—not always an easy thing to do for a state political party in constant need of funds, especially at the risk of alienating someone who really might be good for it "next week." But the tactic generally worked, and somehow most people who said they would have it "next week" could, in reality, come up with it "this week" when we insisted it was either that, or we simply could not allow them at the event.

With a little money in the bank and the RNC and Bush teams moving in, the stage was set for the most aggressive campaign West Virginia had ever witnessed from the Grand Old Party.

7

One day is like a thousand years

By late fall of 2003, it became clear that the RNC was serious about holding on to West Virginia for George W. Bush. On November 30, the *Washington Post* ran a story detailing the Bush campaign's massive state-by-state planning. "Our goal is for the largest grassroots effort ever," it quoted Ken Mehlman, the Bush Campaign Manager.

West Virginia was clearly a state targeted for money and organization. In addition to Mary Diamond, GOTV Director Ward Baker, and the new Bush in-state Executive Director, Brian Donahue, the RNC and Bush campaign staffs in the state would grow by leaps and bounds. (Ward Baker was soon another casualty of West Virginia, and he fled back to the comfy confines of Mississippi, replaced by an efficient and hardworking GOTV director named Adam Feldman.)

Our new headquarters was quickly filling up, more than justifying the effort Kris and I had made to secure it. In addition to our permanent staff members, Mary Diamond and Adam Feldman required separate offices. Brian Donahue eventually would be working out of a newly rented Bush headquarters in downtown Charleston—the Bush campaign did not want the President so identified with the state Republican Party that its new Executive Director actually worked out of GOP headquarters—but for now he and his own growing staff were leasing our offices, and our level of onsite activity was quickly taking an immediate upturn.

The myriad of things a State Party deals with can sometimes be mind boggling. Finding candidates, raising money, keeping various factions united, mollifying donors, working with the National Party, responding to the media—these daily duties and more keep Party staff members on their toes.

Several events during just a few days in December 2003 offered some perfect examples.

◆   ◆   ◆

One morning early that month, Kris placed a call to me, telling me he had just gotten off the phone with Don Blankenship, the CEO of Massey Energy, and the man most responsible for our new headquarters. Despite his generosity, Blankenship rarely asked for anything, but this day he had informed Kris that he was about to lay off more than 400 workers because of a longstanding delay in getting permits approved through the Army Corps of Engineers office in Huntington. Blankenship was angry, said Kris, and made no bones about the fact that if the layoffs occurred, the blame was going to be placed squarely at the feet of the Bush Administration.

Just the previous week, Bush had taken a pretty heavy hit in northern West Virginia when he lifted the steel tariffs, and more bad news on coal layoffs was something the President could scarcely afford in the southern regions of West Virginia. Even then, I knew the Bush folks would be unlikely to offer any assistance, but I recommended that Kris call Darren Bearson in the White House Political Department, and make sure Bearson understood the magnitude of the political fallout that was about to occur. If everything else was in order and the permit holdup was really based on some unnecessary delay, trying to resolve the issue with a simple phone call to the Army Corps of Engineers was worth a try.

The White House had long had a love-hate relationship with Don Blankenship. While Blankenship was a major donor, he was also a persistent critic. I particularly recalled one meeting at our headquarters in early 2003 when Coddy Johnson, then with the White House prior to moving over to the Bush reelection campaign, was giving an Administration update to several of our invited guests from around the state. Blankenship was in attendance, and he dominated the meeting with long monologues telling Coddy everything the Administration was doing wrong. Afterward, Coddy was livid.

Massey was a constant source of controversy in West Virginia, having consistently been fined and penalized for accidents, spills and a variety of environmental violations. The White House always had to tread carefully in regard to Massey Energy. Once, it even scrapped our suggestion that Blankenship be among a group of individuals we selected to greet the President at the airport during one Charleston visit. We never knew whether it was because of the Administration's trepidation at being seen as too close to Massey Energy, or whether it was just a slap at Blankenship personally for what was perceived as his constant griping.

The result of Kris' call to Bearson yielded pretty much what I expected. Bearson lectured Kris on Massey's poor environmental record, and at some point brought up Coddy's name and Blankenship's rude treatment of him. Bearson said the White House could not be seen as doing anything to pull strings for Massey. We were left with little hope of any help for Don Blankenship from Washington.

◆   ◆   ◆

That same day, Dick Stevenson from *The New York Times* called. Al Gore had just endorsed Howard Dean for President, and the *Times*—just like *The Washington Post* two weeks earlier—was trying to gauge whether Dean was too liberal for states like West Virginia. I refused to bite, and gave him the RNC talking points that we expected a tight race regardless of who the Democrats nominated. In fact, Dean *was* too liberal for West Virginia, but the last thing we wanted to create was the perception that if Dean won his Party's nomination, Bush had the election in the bag.

◆   ◆   ◆

Later that afternoon, in a surprising result to most observers, it was announced that the U.S. Supreme Court had upheld the Campaign Finance Reform bill. I did some media interviews with reporters who were asking about the effect it has on State Parties, which is considerable. I could never understand why John McCain, Russ Feingold and others (including, apparently, the Supreme Court) preferred that all the money go to the special interests rather than the national and state parties, where at least it all gets reported. Despite McCain's public outrage toward the "527" groups that sprang up in 2004, they would never have materialized if McCain-Feingold had never reared its ugly head. A lot of people think McCain's motives were to hurt the RNC, because it was so heavily behind Bush over McCain in 2000, and that's not hard to believe.

But while the court decision was a disappointment, we had already grown accustomed to the lack of "soft" money contributions from the RNC, and the ruling simply meant we had to continue finding more ways on our own to raise the funds we needed to accomplish our goals.

◆   ◆   ◆

Despite my efforts to keep the State Party away from the Governor's race and focused on the State Legislature—at least through the Primary—Kris had other ideas. For several days, he had been pushing me to think about how to organize some "candidate forums" for the GOP gubernatorial candidates. I told him it was a bad idea for the State Party to sponsor such events when his brother was one of the candidates. I suggested that the Federation of Young Republicans or the Federation of Republican Women might be a good group to tackle such an undertaking. But the last thing we needed was to get our staff tied up in all the hassle and arrangements of putting on a series of debates when what we needed to focus on was the training of our State legislative candidates, County Chairs and grassroots activists.

Kris would not be dissuaded, though. He asked me to draft a letter for him to send gauging the interest of the various candidates in participating in these forums, which Kris envisioned as a series of five held at various locations all across the state.

Clearly, to me, this was an effort to aid his brother, and was probably Monty's idea. Monty was having trouble raising money, and needed something to increase his profile. Monty was a good public speaker, and a quick thinker. A debate was right up his alley. If I was Monty Warner's campaign manager, I would consider it a great idea. But the State Party didn't need to be seen as staging events for the benefit of the Chairman's brother, and almost anything we did in regard to the Governor's race would be perceived as such, legitimately or not. I had already convinced Kris to send a mass email, promising people that we were staying out of the Governor's race until a candidate was chosen in the Primary. Now, contrary to that promise, Kris wanted to organize debates, or, as he preferred to call them, "forums."

I knew Kris was under constant personal and financial strain from his family and his business (literally one and the same) due to undertaking the Chairman's position in the first place. If Monty was pushing Kris to organize the "forums," I could understand how Kris could tell himself, hey, it's the Party's job anyway. But the strain of dealing with all the demands was beginning to show on him.

I admired Kris and wanted him to succeed, and I tried to redirect him whenever I could back to an overall focus on his own stated goal—taking over the State Legislature—and away from any other side issues, including the Governor's race and the Presidential campaign.

◆   ◆   ◆

As 2003 drew to a close and the all-important 2004 campaign loomed before us, I needed have a heart-to-heart with Kris on several important items, including:

- Fundraising. We needed to hire a full time receptionist so we could free Olivia, who was doing double-duty, to focus solely on raising money.

- Media relations and message. I wanted Kris to quit worrying about who was being quoted. If this was truly a Party of principle and not personalities, it should not have mattered. My media background was one of the main reasons I was hired, and we needed to take advantage of it. Plus, we needed to make sure our message was delivered in such a way that we were gaining Democrat votes, not losing them. If Kris had been good with the media, I would have been happy to always let him do interviews. The problem was, so many of his interviews contained comments that were potential landmines.

- Staying focused. We needed to stay out of the Bush campaign except when they asked us for something, and stay out of the Governor's race until our nominee was chosen in May.

- Attitude, example. We needed to do a better job of obeying Ronald Reagan's 11th Commandment, and not speak ill of fellow Republicans, even privately. Too often, we fell into a trap of badmouthing our fellow Republicans, and we needed to elevate our tone.

I also needed to discuss pay raises for the staff, and time off during the upcoming holidays. Kris had a work ethic second to none, and while he never argued about vacations or days off, I knew it went against his natural inclinations.

Kris and I finally had a chance to meet in mid-December. His mood was upbeat, and we breezed through each issue without much trouble. He was agreeable on everything I proposed, including pay raises and time off, but he still wanted to pursue the gubernatorial debates. He agreed that the State Party would not be the sponsoring organization, but still wanted to pursue the idea of one of our affiliate organizations running with the ball and setting up a series of debates.

So far, he told me, only Dr. Doug McKinney and brother Monty had replied and accepted the debate idea. I figured Larry Faircloth, the House of Delegate member, would accept as well, but I had doubts about Dan Moore and Rob

Capehart, although of the two, Capehart was the most likely to accept because he was a good speaker, quick on his feet and would probably be confident that he would win any match-up with the rest of the field.

◆   ◆   ◆

In the meantime, I appeared on Hoppy Kercheval's statewide radio program to talk about Howard Dean. The RNC asked me to take a slam at Dean, who, on the *Today* show the previous morning, had said something to the effect that the issues of guns, abortion, gay marriage, etc., were items most southern voters would just have to disagree with him on. The goal was to let voters know of Dean's comments, and paint him as out of touch with most mainstream voters.

I did the show, and made the appropriate points, but I felt awkward doing so. On the one hand, the Bush folks never wanted to give the appearance that they hoped Dean was the candidate. They always wanted us to stress that we expected a tough race no matter which candidate the Democrats nominated. On the other hand, they wanted us to paint Dean as an out-of-touch liberal who could not be elected. It was a tough tightrope to walk. The fact the RNC and Bush campaign were willing to begin attacking Dean—or at least ask its surrogates to do so—apparently meant they, too, thought Dean was the favorite to win the nomination, even five weeks before the first Primary. I had to wonder, are the Democrats really that stupid?

◆   ◆   ◆

There was another annoyance to deal with before year's end. After several days of discussions, Kris and I agreed to issue a press release disavowing Joe Oliverio's GOP campaign for Governor. Oliverio was a painting contractor from Clarksburg who was making outrageous and ridiculous statements. He said in one interview that he was going to auction off a Humvee, and turn southern West Virginia into a drive-through zoo, that type of nonsense. Trouble is, the media kept giving him a lot of play for his ludicrous comments, and we felt it necessary to disavow his campaign because we had no intention of inviting him to any debates or forums with our legitimate candidates. Just the week before, Oliverio's campaign manager quit—and went to work for Oliverio's estranged wife, who announced *she* was running for Governor. (I couldn't make this stuff up.)

Shortly after our press release disavowing Oliverio's campaign hit the wires, Oliverio announced he was switching parties and running for Governor as a

Democrat. The Associated Press reported that Oliverio faxed a precandidacy registration form indicating he'd made the change with the Secretary of State's office. State Democrat Chairman Mike Callaghan surprised me by welcoming Oliverio into his Party, saying the Democrats had the state's "largest political tent." I was absolutely shocked at Mike Callaghan's lack of political savvy on the issue. In response, we issued a press release saying in part:

> *"It's one thing to be proud of having a big tent," said Warner. "It's another when you're proud that the only thing going on inside that tent is a zoo run wild. I guess Joe Oliverio and Mike Callaghan have a lot in common—Joe wants to turn half the state into a zoo, and Mike wants that zoo inside his tent."*

Even some who weren't necessarily always on our "team" were stupefied at Callaghan's open-armed welcome of Oliverio. One of our quick-to-criticize Republican State Senators dropped me an email saying, "I can't believe Callaghan let himself get caught like this!!! I was so glad a few years ago when Joe Oliverio switched to Democrat—I kidded the Democrats about it and then we got him back and now they have him back! You know who the loser is in this??? Mike Oliverio!!! You know Mike has a brother named Joe Oliverio so people associate 'the' Joe Oliverio either as Mike Oliverio or as his brother."

The Senator was referring to Democrat State Senator Mike Oliverio, who had earlier declared his candidacy for Secretary of State. For sure, anyone named Oliverio—and there were a lot of them in northern West Virginia—must have been pulling their hair out.

Within hours, though, another AP story moved on the wire reporting that the Secretary of State's office had ruled that Joe Oliverio could not switch his registration since state law required any such switch to occur at least 60 days prior to the filing deadline. Therefore, Oliverio said, "Since neither Party seems to want me, I'll start the most powerful independent Party this state's ever seen." He said he would call it the "Wild and Wonderful Party." Good luck, Joe.

◆   ◆   ◆

The Bush campaign held a conference call that same evening designed to formally introduce Brian Donahue as the new Executive Director of the West Virginia Bush effort, and to talk about the campaign's plans in regard to West Virginia. There were 40 or 50 "steering Committee" members from around the state on the call, which was led by Congresswoman Capito, Bill Phillips, Coddy

Johnson and Donahue. National Bush Chairman Marc Racicot was on the call as well and offered some words of encouragement. Part of Phillips' job was to introduce Donahue, as well as recognize Kris and Buck Harless. He hurried past Kris' name as fast as he could, offering no supportive comments, and actually made a more detailed and complimentary introduction of our RNC National Committeeman, Bill Pauley, commending Pauley for his work in 2000.

One item discussed was the fact that the Bush Steering Committee was being rolled out state by state to much media fanfare, and the date for West Virginia's rollout was January 5th. At the conclusion of the call, it was interesting that Buck Harless made a point of stressing how much support from the Democrats would be necessary for a Bush victory, a comment quickly amen'd by Phillips. I felt the comment was directed straight at the State Party. Afterwards, I warned Brian Donahue that at some point he would be approached and encouraged to persuade the State GOP to lay off certain Democrat legislative incumbents who might support the President. When that happened, the real fireworks would start.

◆   ◆   ◆

Before the year ended, I needed to finally address the issue of the gubernatorial debates to get Kris off the subject and hopefully focused on something important.

Truth be known, there was very little interest in the Republican gubernatorial Primary campaign of 2004 in West Virginia. For one thing, Democrat Joe Manchin had relentlessly used his Secretary of State position to promote himself for the past few years. He was popular even among Republicans, and was seen by almost all unbiased observers as nearly unbeatable. Plus, even some of our own candidates for Governor admitted that the most important race in the state would be the Supreme Court campaign, since the many 3-2 rulings of the state's activist court had long been blamed for the West Virginia's failure to attract business and industry. While a couple of Justices on the court often voted like Republicans, the state had not elected an actual Republican Justice to the court in decades, but this year many factors were coming together to make such a victory possible.

But with Kris relentlessly egging me on to make gubernatorial debates a reality, I handed the ball to Charles Bolen, the Chairman of the state Young Republican club. The Young Republicans are a national group whose members include Republicans age 18 to 40. Charles had done a great job rebuilding the West Virginia chapter after it had fallen into disarray.

Eventually—and after being persuaded that the Young Republicans and not the State Party would conduct the events—all the gubernatorial candidates expressed interest on some level in participating. My goal was to make sure Charles understood how to professionally stage these events, and then get myself, Kris and the State Party completely uninvolved. Charles was excited to take the project on, and rightfully saw it as a great public relations opportunity for his organization.

Now, the staff and I were ready to turn our attention to our ultimate goal—a ballot filled with a Republican running for every seat in the West Virginia Legislature.

8

Bush whacked

In early January, Kris and Ben were on the road trying to nail down prospective candidates, while I was making final arrangements for a mass filing press conference scheduled in just a few short days. Olivia was working the phones, generating as large a crowd as possible for what we hoped would be a big splash in the media.

Coupled with our radio and newspapers ads pushing our legislative agenda (for a January session that would kick off that coming Wednesday) we hoped to steal the attention from the Democrats and make them feel some heat, both with a full slate of candidates ready to take them on, and a bold legislative agenda that would make good campaign fodder even if they ignored it.

As usually happens, candidates began to step forward now that the filing period was upon us. Two years before, we had fallen short of our goal to fill the ballot. For the 2004 campaign, it looked like it was actually going to happen. Our mass filing event was scheduled for January 12, the first official day of the three-week filing period. Three days earlier, the weather forecast called for freezing temperatures and snow—not an encouraging prediction for a press conference scheduled outdoors around the Lincoln statue at the foot of the Capitol Building. But the day dawned warmer and dry, and more than 70 of our 100-plus committed candidates made the trip to Charleston for the 2 p.m. event, about 30 more than had attended the event in 2002.

Editorials appeared in newspapers around the state praising our efforts. The *Charleston Daily Mail* said Republicans represented a "clear departure" from a past many West Virginians wanted to leave behind. The *Martinsburg Journal* said the resurgence of the state GOP would mean "better candidates from which to choose in both parties." And a news story in the *Beckley Register-Herald* said our effort was designed to "emancipate" West Virginia from decades of Democrat rule.

The idea behind holding a "mass filing" was to show, on the first official filing day, our strength in numbers, and put the Democrats on notice that they were facing competition. But most importantly, we wanted to generate some good, positive press. We met all those goals, but we were still short about 12 candidates to fill the 117 House and Senate seats up for grabs. The rest of the month was spent in a focused drive toward candidate recruitment.

On Monday, January 19, former Republican Governor Cecil Underwood finally announced he would not seek the office again in 2004. Underwood had toyed with the idea of another run, but to our relief, the former Governor—now in his 80s—finally made an official announcement that he was sitting this one out. A reporter for the MetroNews radio network called me and asked for a response. He was trying to put together a package for the 5 p.m. news, and it was already about 10 minutes until 5. Knowing the reporter was pressed for time, I did the interview, but I knew Kris would be upset that I didn't track him down to let him do it. Sure enough, the next day Kris—who had heard the report with my comments on the radio that morning—again "reminded" me that he would prefer to do such interviews. I began to explain why I had done the interview instead of handing it to him, but he quickly cut me off and said he didn't need me to respond.

Okay.

These piques of ego that occasionally struck Kris were constant sources of aggravation. Still, I was pretty good at compartmentalizing them and just moving on. Despite his quick mood swings, when it came down to it I liked and admired Kris, I understood the pressures he faced, and was determined to stay positive and focused through the election.

By mid-January, our goal of filling the ballot by the January 31st deadline was so close we could taste it. Each day, another new candidate was stepping forward to answer the call, sometimes after we made a promise of a quick contribution as soon as they opened a campaign account. The pledge of a few hundred or a thousand dollars to get them off to a good start didn't hurt in the persuasion process.

Financially, we were in better shape than at any time in the two-plus years since Kris became Chairman. Our fundraising had taken a quick upswing as the New Year dawned. Our membership mailings were yielding record results, due in no small part to the fact we had turned to a new mail vendor who managed to add thousands of additional names through list rentals, and do more production and mail for us at a smaller cost than our previous vendor. Several new large dollar donors were coming through for us earlier rather than later, and that helped as well.

During the final week of the filing period in late January, Kris and I attended the RNC Winter Meeting in Washington D.C. We both agreed that we seldom learned anything helpful during these three-day sessions held twice each year (nearly everything they covered had already been shared with us in various emails), but the RNC wanted us to be there, and we were constantly trying to stay in the good graces of the RNC and the Bush campaign. Kris and I were in frequent contact with Ben back in West Virginia, where he and Olivia were working the phones, following up leads, and practically turning over rocks to find Republicans willing to seek a state House or Senate seat. When we returned from Washington late on the day before the filing deadline, we were down to just two races that needed to be filled.

Through arm-twisting, promises of campaign contributions, and any other means of cajoling them we could think of, we nailed down our final candidates on the morning of the filing deadline. Kris, Ben, Olivia and I were looking at each other, waiting for someone to find a district tucked away somewhere that we had missed. We examined and re-examined our list of candidates, making sure we had left no holes, wondering aloud about candidates who had previously committed but who had not contacted us for a while. We made some phone calls to our "committed" list just to make sure they were still on board. Everyone was.

That evening, Kris took the staff to a local steakhouse for a congratulatory dinner. It was the strangest of celebrations. Everyone was too exhausted to show the excitement we felt inside. I leaned back in my chair and looked across the table at Ben and Olivia. I thought about how proud I was of these two young, dedicated employees.

Ben had worked so hard to fill the ballot. He had tracked down every lead, made countless phone calls, traveled literally thousands of miles across the state. He was often exhausted, and sometimes his temper flared when one more thing was added to his plate. But he had been personally devoted to our goal. Each of us had worked hard on the task, and could each claim credit for finding candidates here and there. But our success in filling the ballot was due more to Ben's hard work than anyone else, and I was as happy about filling the ballot for Ben's sake as I was about the accomplishment itself.

One of Ben's greatest attributes was his loyalty. No one was more troubled by Monty Warner's entry into the Governor's race than Ben. He had been personally loyal to Kris ever since we hired him, but since Monty had made his gubernatorial aspirations known, I had seen Ben for the first time begin questioning Kris' motives. I "talked him down" more than once, and reassured him that there was little chance of Monty winning our Primary. After that, it wouldn't be an issue anymore.

For her part, Olivia was just as admirable an employee. Hired as a fundraiser, she was always performing many other duties as well, always without complaint. She had jumped in to help Ben with phone calls and contacts as the filing deadline neared and Kris and I were away at the RNC meeting. She worked long hours, and did anything necessary to advance the Party's goals.

I had been managing people for 20 years, and often saw young employees who let their love of the nightlife or their lack of personal discipline negatively affect their work life. Ben and Olivia were both young, attractive, single people who were just starting their careers. While they both had lots of friends and an active social life, they stayed focused on their duties, and I was very proud of them both.

Over the next few days, the emails, phone calls and letters of congratulations poured in from the Republican faithful around the state. I don't think anyone—including maybe ourselves—thought we could find a Republican candidate for every state House, Senate and statewide race in West Virginia in 2004. But we did it.

Over the next few days, editorials appeared in newspapers commenting on the Republican effort. A good example was the *Martinsburg Journal*, which wrote an editorial on February 4 congratulating us and noting that "from President to surveyor, voters will have choices this year, unlike too many years in the past."

To our delight, another 15 Republican names showed up on the legislative ballot, including many candidates with whom we were completely unfamiliar who had just taken it upon themselves to file for office without even contacting us. In the end, a total of 152 Republicans were vying for 117 available seats. We were actually going to be having more than 20 Primary contests on the Republican ticket—an amazing event in West Virginia. This was a huge accomplishment in a state that often saw half of its legislative races uncontested by Republican challengers, and where the Primary election was usually seen as more important than the General, since the winners of Democrat Primaries were assumed to be locks for victory in November.

In addition, we had filled every race for statewide office with a Republican candidate—Governor, Secretary of State, Agriculture Commissioner, State Treasurer, State Auditor, and the Supreme Court. Brent Benjamin, my Republican attorney friend, and Betty Ireland, a local business professional, had legitimate chances at winning the Supreme Court and Secretary of State races.

Brent actually ended up facing Primary opposition in the form of Huntington attorney Linda Rice, who, it was soon discovered, had actually made a campaign contribution to the Democrat candidate, Supreme Court Justice Warren McGraw, and had only become a registered Republican a few years earlier. I convinced Kris that we should urge our Executive Committee to make an endorsement in the race, an unusual step in the Primary election. In the end, the Committee solidly backed Brent Benjamin, and we purchased radio time to make our endorsement known.

As with most things, though, the glow of our accomplishment was quickly dimmed by another bone of contention with the Bush campaign. Around the first of February, we sent out nearly 20,000 fundraising letters. We were using a new mail vendor, and we were happy with his service and results. But he was also someone who, because of his high volume of work, pressured us to quickly sign off on the letters and designs he composed so he could get them printed and out the door. After a call from the vendor begging us to give the green light, I finally glanced quickly over the text of the latest appeal. It was typical, boilerplate fundraising language, and his previous letter for us had been satisfactory, so I gave the OK and moved on.

A week or so later, a Democrat member of the state House of Delegates was reading our letter in session on the floor of the House. He was accusing Kris Warner of calling Democrats "arrogant and abusive, blustering and belligerent," offering "more of the same sloppy management and shoddy government." The phrase "gross incompetence" was thrown in for good measure. And he was right—that's exactly what the letter said, over Kris Warner's signature.

Frankly, that kind of language, for better or worse, is pretty typical fare for a partisan fundraising letter. But in West Virginia, Kris and I had always been careful to distinguish the Democrat elected leaders—or "Ruling Party"—from rank and file grassroots Democrats, who we were trying to attract. The fundraising letter did not make that distinction very clear.

But the cardinal sin of the letter was that it early on made mention of President Bush. The line about Bush was no big deal—"In just ten short months, Americans will decide whether we continue President George W. Bush's compassionate, conservative agenda, or whether our nation takes a sharp turn to the left…" etc., etc.

It didn't take long for my phone to ring with Bush regional representative Dave DenHerder on the line. Dave blasted me for, a, using the President's name without permission, b, having the President's name in the same letter that blasted Democrats in such harsh tones, and, c, basically being alive and breathing.

"This is not the tone the President wants to take," he admonished. "The President is running a positive, inclusive campaign."

"And so he should," I agreed. "He's the President. But we're a State Party. We're supposed to be partisan. But Dave, I agree with you—we should not have used the President's name in that letter without your permission, and I apologize."

All over the state, Republican enthusiasm was at an all-time high. Because of the efforts of the State Party, our GOP base was energized and ready to make a major move. While everyone except die-hard Democrats were singing our praises, including most newspapers, radio talk shows and TV stations, the one consistent source of complaint and disgruntlement with our efforts was the campaign of the President of the United States—a President we loved and admired. It was often disheartening. But I was beyond losing sleep over it.

I was also amused at the constant message to us from the Bush folks that the President was running a "positive" campaign. On the one hand, nothing negative ever came out of the President's mouth, of course. But on the other, the RNC—with the full assent of the White House—was hammering away in typical political fashion.

Headline from the RNC Web site of February 13, 2004:

"Kerry Unplugged: After 14 years, Kerry changes stories on WMDS; Watch Kerry change his WMD story before your very eyes," followed by news clips of John Kerry's various statements on weapons of mass destruction in Iraq.

Headline from the Bush-Cheney '04 Web site of February 13, 2004:

"Unprincipled, Chapter 1," in regard to John Kerry, with information similar to that found on the RNC site.

Positive indeed. It's OK to call John Kerry unprincipled, but don't call the Democrats in West Virginia arrogant.

Although I always thought the Bush campaign severely overreacted to the fact that the State Republican Party would engage in partisanship (what were we thinking?) I also could somewhat understand why they, from their perspective, would be upset. I had apologized for our grievances, and, while still taking ultimate responsibility, I had explained to Dave that neither Kris nor I had actually composed the letter and were pressured to hurry it out the door. But Dave wasn't finished. He called back a few minutes later and very pointedly requested that no one from the State Party attend a Bush regional public meeting that was scheduled for the next evening in Raleigh County.

I replied, "Sure, no problem." But then I began to do a slow burn. This was over the line. The more I stewed on it, the more infuriated I became. I called Kris to let him know the turn of events, and he was equally appalled at the idea of the State Party being "dis-invited" to a public Bush meeting. Clearly, we were being punished for our transgression, and this time the Bush folks not only wanted to send us a message, they seemed intent on humiliating us as well.

Later that evening, I dashed off the following email to DenHerder:

> *Over the last two years, no one…probably including Shelley (Capito)…has spent more time publicly defending the President in the media and in front of groups, when he has been criticized even from his base for being a "big spending liberal" on Medicare or being soft on immigration or whatever…we always drop everything to jump on the air or in print defending him to the hilt, not only because we believe it's our job, but because we believe in him. We have devoted countless staff hours to RNC programs like voter I.D. and voter reg. Right now, Ben Beakes is on an airplane to Miami for 72-hour training that will cost us money we don't have, but we agreed to it because Randy asked it and we want to be cooperative and supportive. We have done I think absolutely everything requested of us to put our names on press releases the RNC has asked of us blasting Dean or Kerry, or supporting the President's programs. We study the talking points closely and follow them. We have been his biggest cheerleader…so it hurts to be dis-invited to a Bush event.*

OK, I admit I was having a good, old-fashioned hissy fit, but I felt better, anyway. Randy Kammerdiener, our regional RNC rep, called a couple of days later, and, with all good intentions, offered some advice on smoothing things over. He suggested we make sure to limit our attacks to targeted Democrat incumbents by name, rather than attacking the Democrat Party as a whole. This, he said, would mollify the Bush campaign, but still allow us to pursue our goal of winning legislative seats.

I listened and considered what he was saying, but reminded him that our mantra for more than two years has been one variation or another on the fact that "70 years of one-Party rule in West Virginia is enough." I offered to compromise by always referring to the Democrat Party as the "Ruling Party," but he did not seem to think that was good enough. What he and the Bush folks needed to come to grips with was the fact that the horse was already out of the barn. Our candidates were already off and running with the "70 years is enough" campaign, and there was no reigning it in now. Nor did we want to, frankly. The Bush crowd seemed completely out of touch with the sea change occurring politically in West Virginia. To try once more to reason with them, I decided to write a memorandum for them offering my perspective of the landscape in West Virginia for 2004. I concluded the 7-page diatribe by arguing that the day was past when Republicans had to be ashamed of their Party in West Virginia:

While West Virginia is not yet a state where the President can campaign solely as a Republican with the Republican ticket, as though it were a safe Republican state, many signs indicate that West Virginia is trending toward joining its southern brethren as part of the "solid south" for the GOP. Old Democrat loyalties, based primarily on union allegiances, are fading as the influence of the unions fades, due to a dying union population, the continuing loss of union mills, factories and jobs, and the realities of the new economy. Additionally, most newspapers (numerous editorials), radio talk shows and television reports around the state are heralding the Republican resurgence as a positive event, with the notable exception, of course, of the Charleston Gazette. It is quickly becoming acceptable to be a Republican in West Virginia; the Party and its candidates do not have to fear "flying our banner too high," at least no more than in most states at General Election time.

That evening, I saw Brian Donahue, the in-state Bush Executive Director, at a Lincoln Day Dinner in Charleston. I wasn't expecting any response to my unsolicited missive, but Brian brought it up, and said, "Hey, I saw your memorandum. There was a lot of good stuff in there. I haven't had a chance to talk to Dave about it yet, but I will, and I'll get back to you."

"Great," I replied, fully expecting the exact follow-up conversation we eventually had—none at all. The Bush folks had their philosophy for West Virginia, and it was focused on reelecting the President, not on capturing the State Legislature.

The dinner itself that evening was a big success—probably the biggest Lincoln Day Dinner in Kanawha County history, with more than 300 in attendance. Congresswoman Shelley Moore Capito was the guest speaker, and Brian Donahue offered remarks from the Bush campaign. Shelley graciously acknowledged Kris Warner and the work of the State Party, and congratulated us on filling the state legislative ballot, to a huge round of enthusiastic applause. Later, Kris was invited to say a few words, and he carried to the stage a large poster board I had ordered made up listing each of our 172 legislative, statewide and Congressional candidates. Again, he was roundly applauded and commended, and I was glad that Brian Donahue was there to witness the enthusiasm in the room for the State Party's efforts.

But in fairness to Brian, no one in the Bush campaign really doubted that Republicans in West Virginia were much more active, involved and enthusiastic than they were in 2000. And they no doubt understood that the State Party was responsible. Their concern was that the new Republican activity would spur the Democrats to an even greater response, and since the Democrats outnumbered the Republicans—well, you do the math.

As I had outlined in my memorandum, I sincerely believed that Republicans, "Republicrats," Independents and many Republican-leaning Democrats were ready to collectively vote for a new direction in November, and in big enough numbers to offset the hard-core Democrat base. Only time would tell for sure. It was a gamble, but hey, there was really little to lose—except the presidency, of course.

9

Can't we all just get along?

One day in early February, I was scanning the *Charleston Daily Mail* newspaper's Web site, and saw a story headlined, "Byrd wants Bush gone." As I was reading, I was surprised to see comments by Kris Warner. The story quoted Kris as saying that voters saw Senator Robert C. Byrd as "an old, out-of-touch man."

Damn. I knew right away there would be a problem. While the *Daily Mail* did not highlight Kris' quote in its headline, I knew someone would. I called Kris immediately and read him the quote.

"Damnit," said Kris. "Karin Fisher (the *Daily Mail's* Washington-based reporter) asked me that question. She asked me if I thought voters saw Byrd as just an old, out of touch man, and I was just basically agreeing with her."

While I considered it entirely possible that Kris had just let fly with the comment without any prompting, I also knew from experience Karin Fisher's interview style was indeed often leading—basically putting words in your mouth—and you had to be on guard for it. Kris may well have been sucked into the trap.

"I think we need to do a clarification," I said. "Calling Byrd old and out of touch is going to be a story."

Kris quickly agreed. I began working on a press release, but before I was finished, I saw this headline move on The Associated Press wire: "Warner says voters see Byrd as 'old, out of touch.'"

I quickly hurried to put the finishing touches on our "clarification:"

> State GOP Chairman Kris Warner today clarified remarks attributed to him referring to Senator Robert C. Byrd as an "old, out-of-touch man."
> "My remarks about Senator Byrd were made during a lengthy conversation with the reporter, who actually suggested to me that some West Virginians may perceive Senator Byrd in that light," said Warner. "I was basically agreeing with her analysis, but my response was much more focused on Senator Byrd's constant,

partisan sniping at President Bush as opposed to his age. To me, Senator Byrd's age is irrelevant."

Warner added, "I stand by my contention that Senator Byrd is largely out of touch with most West Virginians, especially regarding Iraq, and the 'Anybody but Bush' mentality taking over some of the Democrat leadership."

Added Warner, "I believe that people can be valuable contributors to our society at all stages of life. In fact, I supported my own father for the House of Delegates in 2002, and he was 76."

I rushed it out by fax and email, and made sure it went first to the AP, hoping they would do a re-write and get our fresh comments in their story. To my relief, that happened very quickly, and all the stories that eventually appeared contained Kris' revised remarks clarifying our stance. Still, most papers that ran the story—thankfully, buried inside as opposed to the front page—used the "old, out of touch" comment in the headline.

A few days later, Brian Donahue called to tell me he had received "three different phone calls" from people telling him that Kris' comments had angered Byrd so much that the Senator was redoubling his efforts against Bush in West Virginia. He declined to tell me who the calls came from, which did not surprise me.

"That may be true," I replied. "But Byrd was already galvanized against Bush. He's been planning all along to do everything possible to keep Bush from winning West Virginia again."

"I know that," said Brian. "But we don't have to give him any new ammunition."

I continued to downplay Brian's concerns, and said, "Brian, I know what you're saying, but I disagree with any effort to blame the State Party for causing Byrd to work harder against Bush. He was already planning to do that."

I was determined to defend our position, but in my heart I agreed with Brian, at least to a degree. Kris' quote amounted to giving Byrd more logs for his fire.

Shortly after my conversation with Donahue, I got a call from Richard Benito at *USA Today*. He was attempting to track down Kris for a story on how State Chairmen were viewing the Presidential race so far. John Kerry had surpassed Howard Dean as the Democrat frontrunner—Dean had famously imploded, as many predicted he would—and Benito was looking for state-by-state reactions.

Afraid of another disastrous quote emerging from Kris' lips, I convinced Benito that I spoke for the Party, and he agreed to do the interview with me. I stayed close to the "talking points" on Bush, and refused to discuss John Kerry specifically on the grounds that Kerry was not yet the official Democrat nominee. Immediately afterward, I emailed Brian Donahue, Dave DenHerder and Mary

Diamond to let them know the interview had taken place, along with a brief description of what was asked, and what had been my replies. I also added this:

> *I think that's about it...although, of course, I mentioned that Robert Byrd is old and out of touch. (Do I have to say I'm just kidding?)*

Mary Diamond, who was in D.C. at the time for an RNC staff meeting, wrote back and said, "I'm laughing, but I wonder if the Bush boys are." I thanked her for her sense of humor, and added that a sense of humor was something the Bush boys could use.

◆   ◆   ◆

Our first candidate-training seminar was fast approaching. I had lined up Mark Weaver, a brilliant strategist from Ohio, to once again be the featured presenter. Mark, who had run the successful campaign for Betty Montgomery in the 1994 Ohio Attorney General's race, been heavily involved in Ohio Governor Bob Taft's campaigns, as well as many other campaigns in Ohio and elsewhere, was a teacher by profession and had wowed our candidates at an earlier seminar we had conducted.

Prior to the seminar, though, I needed to meet with Craig Blair. Blair was a first-year member of the House of Delegates from a mostly Republican district in the Eastern Panhandle who had sold water softeners door to door for 20 years and was a shoo-in when he ran for the House in 2002. Because his election was assured, Blair raised no money on his own, instead helping other candidates in his region. Craig Blair, in his early 40s, was an energetic ball of fire. His mind was constantly exploding with ideas, and his enthusiasm was contagious. He was a big cheerleader for the State Party, and we counted him among our closest allies.

However, Craig also considered himself an expert on campaigning, despite having run only one race—and one he was assured of winning, at that. Craig's exuberance was to be admired, but his ideas on campaigning were typical of newcomer thinking. Banners, yard signs, fliers—to Craig, these were the keys to success. Craig was an expert marketer, no doubt about it, and a skilled computer design artist. But he made the mistake of many novice candidates in thinking that intricate, well-designed yard signs and banners were the keys to victory when, if fact, the only thing that matters on yard signs is that the candidate's last name is as large and visible as possible.

Craig had come to our October training seminar, but not in time to hear much of Mark Weaver's presentation. When we gave Craig some time to speak at the end of the day, he had rolled out his yard signs and banners and proclaimed that devices like these would help all candidates win—a message in direct conflict with what our candidates had just learned from Weaver. I was determined not to let that happen again, and a few days before our upcoming seminar, I asked Craig to stop by the office for a chat.

As I began to explain my concerns, as gently as I could, Craig interrupted and said, "Don't worry, I'm not going to contradict what Mark Weaver says." But in the next breath, he added, "However, I have some things I'm going to say that I know will help these candidates."

"Craig," I replied, "you've run one campaign. You have to give me a little credit. I've been doing this full time for eight years. I've been involved in hundreds of campaigns. I've learned from the best. I'm no genius on my own, but do you have any idea how many RNC and other campaign seminars I've been to? The whole reason I'm bringing in Mark Weaver to do this seminar is because he's been running successful campaigns for 20 years. He's the best, and he knows what works."

"Kiss my ass!" Craig blurted out, shifting quickly to the edge of his seat. "Listen. No one has more at stake than I do in this election."

"How do you figure that?" I asked.

"Because, I didn't get elected to serve in the minority. I'm going to be part of the majority Party, if I have to get us there myself."

Craig and I went around for several more minutes, and a few more exclamations of "kiss my ass" came my way. Normally, with almost anyone else, I would have ended the meeting the first time that phrase was used. But I liked Craig immensely. I knew his fiery personality was often beyond his control, but would soon be tempered.

Eventually, I convinced Craig that since this was indeed the West Virginia Republican Party's campaign training seminar, we had a right to control what was said and taught. I had to present this in a fashion that he would accept, but without angering him to the point that he would refuse to attend—which would have sent a bad message to his fellow GOP Legislators and all our candidates, many of whom already knew him and knew of his support for us.

We parted cordially, but I knew some of my words had stung. Craig was a proud, sensitive man, and had put himself on the line several times for his own beliefs, as well as in support of the State Party, even when other Republicans were upset at us. Trying to temper the well-intentioned but bad advice our freshmen

Delegates and Senators wanted to offer to new candidates, while at the same time keeping them on our team, was often a tightrope act.

The seminar itself was a big success. More than 130 of our candidates and campaign volunteers attended, and Mark Weaver was accorded a standing ovation at the conclusion of his four-hour presentation. Craig Blair told me later he thought Mark was very good. I think he learned a lot that day, as he sat there listening painfully to Weaver minimize the importance of Craig's passions—yard signs, banners and Web sites.

I did set aside the last hour of the session for an open question and answer session between candidates and incumbents. The hour offered a perfect example of why we needed professional training for our candidates—as opposed to depending on training by our State Legislators—when one of our House of Delegates members offered this pearl of wisdom to our candidates: "Wherever you go, in parades or events, make sure to play a lot of Toby Keith music. Everybody loves Toby Keith."

You just can't buy astute advice like that.

Meanwhile, Democrats in the State Senate were once again blasting away at President Bush. Our Senate GOP leader, Vic Sprouse, did a great job on Hoppy Kercheval's morning radio show condemning this tactic, which, he noted correctly, was obviously orchestrated by the DNC. I wrote a press release condemning the effort as well, and made sure to run it by the RNC, since it mentioned the President. To my surprise, they approved it with only a couple of minor changes (they weren't fond of my sentence that the "Ruling Party was fiddling while Rome burned"). Still, I was pleasantly surprised that they approved us taking a swipe at the Democrats for taking a swipe at the President.

The heat we were putting on the Democrats in the Legislature was clearly taking a toll. Never seriously challenged before, they reacted with a mixture of anger and confusion. Will Rogers once joked, "I belong to no organized political Party. I'm a Democrat." In West Virginia, that fact was all too obvious. During one contentious Legislative Committee meeting, lacking the votes they needed, Democrats got up and fled the room rather than face a losing vote. The *Charleston Daily Mail* story was headlined, "Democrats walk out to avoid vote," and compared it to the Texas Democrats fleeing to Arkansas to avoid a redistricting vote in 2003.

Senator Billy Wayne Bailey, caught up in a scandal regarding his "contract" work for a Council on Aging program—a program to which he routinely funneled state money—lashed out at the GOP, calling Kris Warner a "slumlord," and complaining that he could not afford to resign his seat in the Senate because he had a family to feed. Bailey—the same Senator who always made some crack about me being from out of state—also said in the *Beckley Register-Herald* that he was "fed up" with Warner "trying to force the majority Party into the corner," noting that Democrats "govern this state. We've governed this state fair and honest."

I had to laugh out loud. Billy Wayne reminded me of W.C. Fields—"Go away, kid, ya bother me."

10

Trouble is our middle name

In mid-March, we learned that John Kerry—who had basically wrapped up the Democrat nomination—was coming to West Virginia on Tuesday, March 16, in a daylong visit culminating in a "Victory Celebration" at the Civic Center in Charleston. I knew what that meant—a full-scale opposition, or "bracketing" offensive, coordinated by the RNC and carried out by various surrogates, including the State Republican Party.

The media phone calls began coming in at a rapid pace. I did several TV and newspaper interviews, as did Kris. One of Kris' interviews was with The Associated Press, which reported that "West Virginia Republicans" were planning a simultaneous "Support the President Rally," and quoted Kris once again blaming the problems in West Virginia on 70 years of one-Party rule by the Democrats.

Within hours, I received the dreaded phone call from Brian Donahue.

"Gary, I thought Kris' comments were fine, until the end," he said.

"What was wrong with the end?" I asked in faux innocence.

"Well, it's just so partisan," he replied with a heavy sigh.

"Brian," I said, truly weary of this whole debate. "We're just going to have to agree to disagree about that." I was fed up with criticism that the Republican Party was too critical of the Democrats.

He asked me to transfer him to Mary Diamond, and I could only imagine the level of consternation directed at Warner and Abernathy in that conversation.

Soon, I received an email from Dave DenHerder, then from Coddy Johnson. Then Coddy actually went to the trouble to call me, which was a serious development since Coddy was now the National Field Director for the Bush campaign and I seldom heard from him directly anymore.

To my surprise, Coddy was friendly and affable. His only concern was over the story's description of the Bush rally as something put together by "West Virginia Republicans." The Bush folks had gone to great pains to make sure the rally was a "bipartisan" rally for the President, but many press stories automatically assumed (correctly, in reality) that it was a Republican event. After I assured Coddy that neither Kris nor I had described it that way, he was generally satisfied. I told him of Brian's comments about Kris' response in the story that the job loss in West Virginia was due not to the President, but to longtime Democrat control of the Legislature. Coddy said he had no problem with that reply, which I made a point of sharing with Brian in a later conversation.

Coddy, in his own unique way, did manage to convey that we should always talk with Mary Diamond before speaking to the press about the President or the Presidential campaign, and failure to do so "could get the attention of people more important than me," he added ominously.

Wanting to avoid a chastising phone call from the President himself—or worse, Karl Rove—I readily agreed to that stipulation.

Mary Diamond herself could sometimes be a little overzealous and controlling. While she wasn't trying to interfere with our media efforts on state issues, she was, by this time, standing in on every interview I did with television reporters regarding Bush, hovering in the corner with arms crossed and head bowed as though she was parsing in her mind every word I said. I could live with that—I knew she was supposed to report back on all media reports on the President or John Kerry—but in my most recent interview she had actually begun to feed me lines in front of the reporters. That was demeaning, embarrassing, and was not something I would tolerate. I had been working in and with the media for more than 20 years. I did not need Mary's help, or oversight, and Randy agreed.

I liked Mary. She was often under a lot of pressure herself from the constant directives from D.C. But she could wear her emotions on her sleeve, and would often engage in animated lectures to Kris or me about staying on the "message of the day." Neither of us was amenable to lectures. Mary even tried to control comments made by our candidates or grassroots volunteers, but she was fighting a losing battle on that front.

While Monty Warner was by this time not someone from whom I was getting a lot of laughs, I had to chuckle at a story Kris relayed to me after the recent Bush counter-rally. Apparently, Mary had jumped down Monty's throat, complaining about Monty doing a TV interview during the rally (which was supposedly unfair since Monty was a gubernatorial candidate). Mary, Kris said, followed Monty onto the elevator, to the parking lot, and all the way to his car, jabbering all the while as Monty kept walking stoically without acknowledging her presence. Kris said Mary was still carrying on dramatically when Monty closed his car door and drove away.

"President Bush is my President, too," Monty said later, with the defiant attitude of a career military officer. "I'm not going to let anyone tell me what I can say about my President—a President I work for, vote for, and support." While I understood that point of view, Monty's strong will and stubborn determination to be his own man would cause countless problems in the months ahead. But for now, with little concern that Monty would actually win the Primary, it was merely an occasional annoyance and in this instance a nice foil to Mary Diamond's sometimes frantic overreactions.

The Bush campaign had not, of course, invited Kris to have a speaking role at their counter-rally—we couldn't have a Republican Party Chairman so visible at a "non-partisan" Bush event—but Senator Vic Sprouse's comments, as reported in the media, made up for that, and must have made the Bushies wince. Vic read a top-10 list of reasons Kerry was wrong for West Virginia, and concluded by saying West Virginians who supported Kerry were "the same ones who have run this state's economy into the ground for 70 years."

I loved it.

◆   ◆   ◆

In mid-March 2004, we held our biannual State Executive Committee meeting. The Executive Committee is officially the governing board of the State Party, and in Ohio was comprised of only 66 members—a man and woman from every State Senate district. In West Virginia, the State Committee had grown to an unwieldy 140-plus members, through various at-large appointments and the decision to make every County Chairman an official voting member of the Committee. Early on in Kris' tenure, it was often a battle just to get enough members together for a quorum. But by 2004, the Committee was energized and anxious, and attendance of 100 or more was not unusual. Still, it was like herding cats, and trying to conduct business with any sense of unity—especially in the early days—was often a challenge.

The March meeting went relatively well. By this time, the Committee was solidly in our corner and supportive of all our efforts, with the typical exception of five or six members who could always be counted on to oppose almost everything. Even Monty's candidacy was not raising too much of a stir, since he seemed like a long shot to win the May Primary and it would all be over and behind us after that. Our main objective was the passage of a bylaws amendment offered by Bob Fish, a Vice Chairman of the Committee and a parliamentary expert.

Each State Party has a man and woman who, along with the State Chairman, make up the membership from each state of the Republican National Committee. Ideally, the National Committeeman and Committeewoman are among the most active and supportive members of the State Party. They should be at the forefront of fundraising, candidate recruitment and all other Party activities. Conversely, many RNC members themselves viewed the position as ceremonial and sought it out only for its prestige. They did little more than attend RNC meetings and dinners and pose for pictures with the President and other dignitaries, bragging at every State Party meeting about how privileged they were to be in such heady company.

Bob Fish offered an amendment spelling out the residency requirements of Committee members, including the National Committeeman and Committeewoman, an issue that had come to the forefront due to the fact that our National Committeeman had months earlier moved out of state, but would not resign his position. Since he was retiring anyway at the end of his term—which concluded after the National Convention in September—it was a moot point in terms of having any affect on him.

But another part of the amendment raised the most controversy. The amendment stated that National Committee members should perform various duties at the direction of the Chairman. That sent Donna Boley, a State Senator and our current National Committeewoman, into a tizzy. She complained that the National Committee members were basically equal to the Chairman in stature, and did not need to follow his directives.

"When we attend RNC meetings," she said, "the RNC makes no distinction between the State Chairman and members of the National Committee."

She was right to a degree, but how the RNC viewed things was not the point. Our State Executive Committee elected one Chairman and one Chairman only, and all State Committee members, including the man and woman we elected to the National Committee, needed to recognize the Chairman's unique leadership position.

In the end, the Committee voted in favor of the amendment by about a 2-1 margin, and Senator Boley left the meeting in a huff.

◆   ◆   ◆

There was a battle brewing to replace our National Committeeman, with former State Chairman David Tyson pitted against Jim Reed, the oil and gas businessman who had been so financially supportive of the Party since Kris became Chairman. I liked both of them, and knew that either one would be an improvement over the status quo. But so far, no one had stepped forward to challenge Donna Boley for National Committeewoman, although we knew there were a couple of women on the Committee who could defeat her if they placed their names in nomination. With Kris' consent, I called Julia Long in Raleigh County, the wife of one of our best county chairmen and a great activist on her own, and asked her to consider running for the position. She was initially taken aback by the suggestion, but she seemed to warm to it as we talked, and said she would give it consideration.

The election would take place at our State Convention in early June—another planning nightmare that was little more than an unneeded headache as far as I was concerned. Some states held conventions, and others did not. Ohio was in the latter category, so I had never been through one before. While it did provide an opportunity to rally the troops yet again, the planning and logistics required countless hours of staff time—time better spent working with our candidates. On top of that, former Chairman David Tyson, who should have known better, had suggested during the State Executive Committee meeting that the Committee hold another meeting in the Fall, right before the election, and someone else suggested it be held in the Eastern Panhandle.

As Kris nodded his assent, I made my way to the podium and was granted permission to interrupt.

"If you want to hold a meeting in the Eastern Panhandle in the Fall, that's fine," I said. "But I think that folks from the Panhandle should take the lead in organizing the meeting." A couple of County Chairmen from that region quickly volunteered to do so, but after the meeting and for several of the ensuing days, I tried to quash the idea. Again, by that time we would need to be solely focused on campaigning, not on staging another Committee meeting. I found an ally in Delegate Craig Blair, who served from the Panhandle and said he would help discourage the idea of another meeting.

Soon, our attention would be distracted again—the big guy was coming to town. In late March, just a couple of days after our Executive Committee meeting, the new RNC Get-Out-the-Vote Director in West Virginia, Adam Feldman, let it slip to Ben Beakes that he heard the President was coming to West Virginia within a week or two. Kris was peeved that the Bush campaign had not informed us officially, but by now we were accustomed to being in the doghouse and didn't think much about it. Kris, though, found out through his own contacts that the President indeed was scheduling a West Virginia trip for Friday, April 2, including stops in Charleston and maybe Beckley.

I was happy that Beckley was possibly on the schedule. Since being elected, Bush had never appeared in West Virginia anywhere outside Shelley Moore Capito's 2nd Congressional District, and the fact he was venturing into the 3rd District would be good for our candidates in southern West Virginia, including our Congressional candidate there, Rick Snuffer, who was taking on longtime Democrat incumbent Nick Joe Rahall.

I had expected that the President would come in close on the heels of John Kerry's appearance. As it turned out, though, the President was actually visiting Huntington, a city on the Ohio-Kentucky border, and the trip was purely "official" in nature—no overt campaigning, just a town hall setting with just a few hundred invited guests to talk about job training.

The official nature of the visit took a lot of pressure off us, and I was glad for that. It let me focus on an issue much more urgent for the purposes of accomplishing our major goal—winning the State Legislature.

◆   ◆   ◆

Around the first of March, the scandal broke in southern West Virginia regarding the salary paid to the director of the Wyoming County senior services center, who, it was discovered was making more than $400,000 a year for heading up the non-profit center. But more importantly for our purposes, one of the director's employees was Democrat Senator Billy Wayne Bailey, one of our most vocal opponents. Bailey was being paid $22,000 per year as a "contract" employee, but of more interest was the fact he was also directing thousands of dollars a year in state money to the Wyoming agency for which he worked, a clear conflict of interest. Also, the Speaker of the West Virginia House of Delegates, Bob Kiss, served as the Wyoming senior services attorney.

On top of that, House Education Chairman Jerry Mezzatesta—long regarded as one of the most arrogant and bullying members of the Legislature—had been caught drawing his $60,000 a year salary from the Hampshire County School District while simultaneously serving in the House of Delegates. Further, Mezzatesta had racked up well over $20,000 in travel expenses. It was also revealed that he had tried to use his position as a member of the House of Delegates to direct a state grant to his school district, directly contrary to an agreement the district had made to the state Ethics Commission when it had originally hired Mezzatesta. Finallly, *The Charleston Gazette* revealed that Mezzatesta's wife was working for him in the Legislature, an arrangement expressly forbidden by state law.

Then, the *Gazette* reported that Democrat Senator Mike Ross had voted for $750,000 for a professional tournament at a golf course where he owns land, after loaning the owner of the course "a substantial amount" of money two years ago to keep the project alive. Ross said it was more than $1 million, but declined to give a specific amount. Again, the clear disregard for any reasonable standard of ethics was appalling.

There was a growing sense that the ball of twine was starting to unravel for the Democrats.

But the *Gazette* could not, of course, attack the Democrats without trying to find something on a Republican. Sensing that Monty Warner was making progress in the Governor's race, and having endorsed the more liberal and local mayor Richie Robb in the GOP Primary, the *Gazette* set its sights on the Warners.

Beginning in early May and over the course of a week, the *Gazette* blasted the following headlines—the first two on the front page, the last on the front of the B section:

"GOP chief's family properties showing tax irregularities."

"GOP chief helped telemarketer accused of fraud."

"Philippi residents upset with GOP chief."

Aside from clear evidence of an unimaginative headline writer, the stories were indicative of the worst kind of "gotcha" journalism. I had a lot of respect for Scott Finn, the *Gazette* reporter writing the stories. I didn't know for sure, but I felt Finn must have been working under a directive from his bosses to find something on the Warners. While there could have existed many legitimate issues to be raised regarding the Warner family, the subjects the *Gazette* was focusing on were benign.

The so-called "tax irregularities" were nothing more than the fact that a Warner business in the small town of Philippi had not had its taxes reassessed to the level the *Gazette* apparently felt appropriate. The telemarketer issue—once you read the story itself—clearly had nothing to do with the Warners at all, except for the fact they rented office space to the company. The Philippi residents who were "upset" with the Warners turned out to be a couple of tenants out of the more than 6,000 the Warner business had leased to over the course of 23 years.

I've always been a believer in the old axiom that you don't get into a fight with a man who buys his ink by the barrel, but in this case the *Gazette*—especially its editorial board—was so consistently and blatantly anti-Republican that it hardly seemed to matter. I wrote and issued a sarcastic press release about the unfairness of the *Gazette*, even though I knew no news organization would touch it (they seldom go after each other). I made up faux headlines, like, "*Gazette* discovers major scandal—Warner is a Republican!" and several others along those lines, along with fabricated stories blaming Kris Warner for everything from Lincoln's assassination to children questioning the existence of Santa Claus. We sent it to our thousands of email recipients, and also knew that many in the press would get the point and have a chuckle over it. In fact, a couple of friendly *Gazette* reporters called to tell me how much they enjoyed it.

11

Brother vs. Brother

The *Charleston Daily Mail* came out with its gubernatorial poll just a week before the election. On the Democrat side, Joe Manchin was clearly running away with the race. On the GOP side, the *Daily Mail* showed a dead heat between Monty Warner and Rob Capehart, with Dan Moore trailing but within the margin of error. The poll showed a whopping 37 percent of voters undecided.

Moore continued to pour his money into television. Capehart had no money, but had been campaigning for two years and was running a strong grassroots campaign. Warner used his resources the most expediently, flooding Republican homes with targeted direct mail pieces that were graphically appealing and on message.

In the days leading up to May 11, several GOP gubernatorial campaigns, especially Bill Phillips on behalf of Dan Moore, turned up the volume on their accusations that the State Republican Chairman was helping his brother behind the scenes. This was true to a degree—Kris couldn't help but be heavily involved in meetings and discussions with Monty's campaign, and later I learned that he had twisted hard on a lot of arms on Monty's behalf. The accusations also disturbed me because I knew for a fact that the State Party itself was doing nothing more for Monty than for any other candidate. But the Party Chairman seemed heavily involved with Monty's race, and perception is reality. When the media asked about it, though, I pointed out—off the record or on background—that Dan Moore had "kingmaker" Buck Harless and Bush co-Chairman Bill Phillips on his side. How could the Moore campaign complain about Kris and Monty Warner?

But on Primary Election night, my worst nightmare came true. As supporters of various candidates gathered at Party headquarters to await the results, the stage was set for a series of events and decisions that would forever alter the future of the West Virginia Republican Party and set a course for disaster.

It was a tight race, as predicted, but Monty Warner gathered 23% of the vote, to 20% for Dan Moore, and 19% for Rob Capehart. Manchin rolled to victory on the Democrat side with 53% of the vote over Lloyd Jackson and Jim Lees. (Brent Benjamin barely squeaked past Linda Rice in the Supreme Court race, and I was sure our endorsement and radio ad helped give Brent the edge, since voters were unfamiliar with either candidate.)

With his less-than-a-mandate size victory, Monty—and the State Party—had our work cut out for us unifying the Party. We had already announced a Unity Breakfast set for two days after the Primary, and all our candidates had originally agreed to attend. But then, that was when each candidate figured he would be the winner. When the Thursday morning event rolled around, only Mayor Richie Robb showed up to offer his support to Monty—a classy move that for a while increased my respect for the Mayor, who was often one of our most contentious Party members. Capehart was actually on Hoppy Kercheval's statewide radio program that morning, and said all the right things, offering supportive comments of Monty, but his absence at our event was conspicuous. Even more disturbing, though, was Dan Moore's no-show act. Moore's campaign people had assured us the previous afternoon that Dan was still planning to attend, but when he didn't appear I asked Ben to call his house. Dan's wife answered, informed Ben that Dan would not be attending, and then slammed down the phone.

(The only thing that saved us from total embarrassment was the fact that a similar Democrat rally later that morning featured a non-appearance by Lloyd Jackson, Manchin's chief rival. At least the Dems were unable to show any more unity than we did.)

Dan Moore struck me as a nice man—a gentleman, really—but simply a poor candidate, clearly uncomfortable in large gatherings, a poor public speaker with little charisma or political leadership ability. All of that was contradicted by his business success in banking and a large network of automobile dealerships, but retail politics is a different ballgame, and it wasn't a comfortable fit for Dan Moore.

Monty Warner was nothing if not comfortable in group settings. He worked a crowd like a seasoned pro. He had a public persona he was able to turn on and off like a lamp. The private man could be very different, as I knew well and would be reminded of many times in the coming months.

Two days after the election, and after we got through the "unity breakfast," Kris and I held an afternoon meeting with Monty to discuss in what ways we could work with him through the election.

The meeting went about as smoothly as passing a kidney stone. First, we sat through a long discourse by Monty on topics ranging from his desire to run as a team with the rest of the statewide ticket to his Politics 101 instruction, which he diagrammed on a dry erase board as Kris and I sat there in less than rapt attention. Monty proceeded to "instruct" us on the most basic political precepts, such as what the base Republican vote was in West Virginia, and the additional percentage he had to get to win.

I was waiting for him to explain how to make an omelet, but he finally finished his long monologue and asked for any feedback. My only goal in the meeting was to establish ground rules regarding communication and duties between Monty's campaign and the State Party. I knew Monty's "take charge" personality, and I knew that if we didn't establish a framework we would have nothing but daily headaches.

"The important thing to me is that the State Party maintains its autonomy," I began. "It's important that the State Party never become the puppet of any candidate or individual."

I related that one of the main complaints I had always heard from Kris was that the State Party in the past was always under the control of former Governors Arch Moore or Cecil Underwood, and when they left power the State Party crumbled behind them.

Monty was silent for a while, and then made a series of comments that left me taken aback. First, he claimed that he was now the top elected Republican official in the state. I replied that Vic Sprouse or Charles Trump, the Senate and House minority leaders respectively, could each make that claim (as could Congresswoman Shelley Moore Capito), but Monty would have none of it. He was fixated on the idea that he was now the "top dog" Republican in the state—an amazing point of view, given that 77 percent of Republican voters in the Primary had selected someone else.

Next, Monty went on to lecture us that he was now the leader of the Republican ticket, and as long as the State Party's focus was where he thought it should be, there would be no problem.

"But the minute that changes," he intoned, "I'll pull the rug out from under you before you know what hit you."

Monty stormed out of the room, and Kris and I sat speechless. Here was the Republican gubernatorial nominee threatening to pull the rug out from under his own brother, the State GOP Chairman, if the State Party failed to meet his criteria of what it should be doing.

I had originally feared a battle like that if Dan Moore or Rob Capehart had won the nomination. And while I had always had strong reservations about Monty winning, I at least had never feared being threatened with a coup by the Chairman's brother.

"It's a shame," Kris finally said, breaking the silence. "This was a very positive meeting up until the end." I frankly could not recall that any part of the meeting had been positive, and the next day I sent an email to Kris illustrating my concerns about the meeting with Monty.

> *I am still in a state of disbelief about some of the things he said. Of all the GOP candidates for Governor, I never would have guessed that Monty Warner would have been the one to threaten to "pull the rug out" from under us if the State Party was not doing what he thought we should do.*
>
> *I am at a loss as to what he thinks you and I and the staff have been doing for nearly three years now...*
>
> *Getting 25,000 votes out of the nearly 110,000 cast in our Governor's race is not a mandate for Party leadership—it's a sign he has a lot of work to do with the other 80,000 GOP voters. I'm not taking anything away from his victory. It was a legitimate victory and he is to be commended for winning this race against Dan Moore's money and Capehart's experience and longevity on the campaign trail...*
>
> *...After you left the breakfast (unity) meeting, Monty stayed up there forever with the other candidates, and last time I checked on them he had them all gathered in the corner watching him draw his donut diagram. We have brought our team this far, and he should let us do our job, and focus on his own campaign. It's great that he is interested in running as a team with the other Republicans, but when it comes to how to do it, I hope he leaves that to us.*
>
> *Monty should understand that this Party is eager to help him win. This staff wants to beat Joe Manchin. We are eager and anxious to help Monty with that goal. But he will lose any enthusiasm or support from the staff (even if he maintains our efforts just because we are doing our jobs) by taking this overbearing, heavy-handed attitude...*
>
> *...the best thing for him to do is to respect your Chairmanship, respect YOUR staff, respect the success we have had, and consider us partners in his effort—partners who have more knowledge and more day-to-day experience—knowledge and experience that he could learn from if he is willing.*
>
> *I don't have any idea how this will play out throughout the next six months. Hopefully, it will not be an issue. As you said after Monty stormed out, this will likely never come up again. I don't know how much of this you agree or disagree with, and you are in a tougher position dealing with a brother in this situation than someone who is not your brother. Nothing is worth creating bad blood that will last within your family long after everyone is done with this political season. I just wanted to share the fact that this meeting has been heavily on my mind. My hope is that Monty and I can be friends and have a mutually beneficial and productive relationship. That is my goal.*

The following week, Coddy Johnson and Dave DenHerder from the Bush campaign came to town for a variety of meetings, chief among them hooking up with Monty and his Campaign Manager, Dick Leggitt, and Kris and me. Coddy was very skilled at making his points in a way that seemed positive and team oriented. The Bush campaign's concern was with Monty's message as it related to the President. Monty had just been quoted in a local newspaper that rather than riding on Bush's coattails, "President Bush may be riding on my coattails."

While the comment was a typical reflection of Monty's unbridled ego, in this case he said he was making a joke that the reporter took literally. Nevertheless, the Bush folks were concerned. (Not long after, I did an interview with the *Charleston Daily Mail* and had the opportunity to say that our candidates would be riding the Bush coattails—in case there was any doubt.)

◆   ◆   ◆

June 4th arrived, and with it our State Convention in Raleigh County. The Tamarack Convention Center in Beckley was a beautiful, new structure with a modern design and a capacity for about 300 conventioneers in one room. Raleigh County Chairman Joe Long and his wife, Julia, did a great job in making all the on-site arrangements, and our staff generated a large and enthusiastic crowd. All told, more than 500 Republicans attended the Friday night dinner with RNC Chairman Ed Gillespie and the Saturday events featuring Congresswoman Capito, Monty Warner, and RNC presentations on their plans for getting out the vote.

Then, during the Saturday afternoon session, Kris took the podium and announced his nominations for the five Electors for President Bush from West Virginia. In a phone call a few days earlier, Kris had run by me the idea of naming the top five runners-up in the gubernatorial race—Rob Capehart, Dan Moore, Richie Robb, Larry Faircloth and Doug McKinney. Kris thought it would be a great way to help unify them behind Monty.

My reaction was that it was a nice idea, but we had better get some input from the Bush campaign about our Electors. We never discussed it further, and now, in front of hundreds of delegates to the State Convention, Kris announced his nomination of the five runners-up. The delegates in attendance unanimously approved the nominations. Once again, Kris' knee-jerk decision and his growing focus on helping Monty would soon come back to haunt us.

During that same afternoon, as we were hearing speeches from our statewide candidates, word came that Ronald Reagan had passed away. Kris made the announcement, and a hush fell over the packed room. We observed two minutes of silence in the former President's honor.

Monty was the final and featured speaker, and before he was finished he brought on stage with him every county, legislative and statewide candidate for a show of unity. It made for impressive pictures, but later, some candidates were grumbling about being used by Monty without their permission.

The real point of contention during the Convention was the election of our National Committeeman and Committeewoman. Jim Reed handily defeated former Chairman David Tyson for the Committeeman spot, which was fine—either one would do a good job, although I felt badly for Tyson, who believed Kris had promised him his support when Tyson handed over the Chairmanship in 2001. But there were four candidates for National Committeewoman, and none could gain a majority of votes during the first few rounds of balloting. Julia Long, who we had tried to recruit, had declined to run, but had instead recruited Pam Stafford, another strong candidate. Facing a challenge had led Senator Boley to decide not to run at all, which in essence had already accomplished our goal.

In the end, Donna Gosney, the former Executive Director we had fired more than a year before, finally won out over State Senator Sarah Minear, House of Delegate member Cindy Frisch, and Pam Stafford.

I liked Donna personally (a feeling Kris did not share), but she was not going to be the kind of fundraiser we were hoping for in that position. Nevertheless, the Convention overall was deemed by most a great success.

Meanwhile, though, my deepest fears about Monty Warner winning the Primary race for Governor were beginning to come true. From May 11 into mid-June, 90 percent of the conversations and planning Kris approached me with were in regard to Monty's campaign. While Kris continued to publicly say the right things—"We're still focused on winning House and Senate races"—the fact was, his attention soon drifted almost exclusively to the Warner for Governor effort. In fact, Monty wanted, and Kris agreed, for Kris to quietly serve as the de facto Chief of Staff for his campaign, with various campaign workers reporting directly to Kris, albeit below the radar screen.

Rumors began to swirl. While I was in Milwaukee for an RNC meeting, Ben Beakes called to tell me he had received at least three calls from members of the Legislature who had heard that I was leaving the State Party to run Monty's campaign. I assured Ben there was no truth to those rumors, but clearly the concern that Monty's long shot effort to beat Joe Manchin would consume the people and resources of his brother's State Party was spreading quickly.

◆   ◆   ◆

In mid-June, a tragic accident claimed the life of the oldest Warner brother, George "Buffy" Warner. Buffy slipped and fell down the steps of his yacht on the island of Ocracoke, located off the shores of North Carolina. He was found early on the morning of June 11, and with Kris away on vacation, Monty called me early that morning and asked if I would serve as a family spokesman, and I was happy to help. Indeed, the press was already calling for comment and reaction, since Buffy had once been a colorful and well-liked member of the State Senate. Their beloved mother had passed away just a few years earlier, and the tight-knit Warner family was in mourning once again.

For a while, Buffy's death took some wind from the Warner sail, especially Kris, it seemed to me. For a long time, he was quieter, and I didn't hear from him as often. I began to realize, though, that one reason I wasn't hearing from him was that he was devoting more and more of his time to his brother's gubernatorial campaign. Whereas before the Primary, Kris would call me 10 to 20 times a day, I was not hearing from him now more than three or four times daily, and soon even less than that. Indeed, it was a mixed blessing on one hand, but a bad omen in reality.

◆   ◆   ◆

We did have some fun, though. Always brainstorming with Olivia for new fundraising possibilities, I came up with an idea to hold a "Vegas Night," including a performance by the King of Rock'n'Roll. A poorly-kept secret among people who knew me was that I was a devout Elvis aficionado, and in fact performed an Elvis show from time to time with band members from Ohio, an act we had put together five or six years earlier. Due to logistical problems—my residency in West Virginia put a damper on our ability to get together for shows or even rehearsals—we were only doing two or three shows a year by this time, but a concert with the State GOP's Executive Director donning the jumpsuit and wig sounded like fun.

Olivia did herself proud building a big crowd for the event, and I volunteered our own Ben Beakes to put together a standup routine featuring his many impressions of local politicians, including a dead-on "Monty Warner."

My band came in from Ohio, and we had a blast during the Saturday night show. The dance floor was packed with Republican activists, candidates, officeholders and our gubernatorial candidate, who seemed to really cut loose, demonstrating some nifty dance moves as "Elvis" performed his greatest hits.

We raised a few thousand dollars, and the night was a lot of fun for everyone. Unfortunately, it became the last truly good and positive memory from the whole campaign, when everyone seemed relatively happy, content, and united. Everything was about to change.

12

On the brink of disaster

Not long after the Primary, Kris had asked me to brainstorm on ways the State Party could help the Warner for Governor campaign, not an unreasonable question regardless of who our nominee was. I suggested that the State Party could encourage donors who gave to our various candidates—donors limited to $1,000 per person to a State candidate—to give additional money to the State Party, where we could accept not only $1,000 per person into our State account, but another $10,000 per person into our Federal account.

It was standard procedure within nearly all state parties to develop a plan like this, but it all hinged on raising the money first, a caveat I stressed to Kris. With these additional funds, we could hire some inexpensive young staffers who would be available to help all of our candidates through generic GOTV activities. Kris seemed excited about the idea, but I stressed again that it could only happen if we demonstrated the ability to raise the money first—and currently, we were pretty strapped for cash.

A few short weeks later, I came into the headquarters one morning and found two people sitting in a spare office, working away furiously on their lap top computers. I knew them both. Craig Bergman was a computer whiz we had used at the end of the 2002 campaign after he had begun working for our U.S. Senate candidate that year, Jay Wolfe. Wolfe had run out of money, and Bergman had come to us looking for a job for the remainder of the campaign. I hadn't heard from him since that election. The other guy was a phone vendor we had used from time to time for automated calls.

"Hi," I said uncertainly.

"Hi," they replied, smiling awkwardly back at me.

I unlocked the door to my office, turned on my computer, then turned around and marched back into the spare office.

"What are you guys doing here?" I asked.

"Oh, Kris said we could do some work out of here until Monty gets his headquarters set up," one of them replied.

"How did you get in here?" I asked.

"Kris loaned us his key."

I turned around and went back to my office, and I stewed for a little while. I was upset that Kris had not let me know he was giving someone his key to the headquarters. Worse, Kris' key was one of only two master keys—keys that would open any door in the headquarters, including my office.

I called Kris and asked him what was going on. He apologized for not letting me know they would be in the headquarters, and explained that they would be working for Monty. He said he would immediately ask for the key back; he forgot it was a master key.

OK, no problem. I accepted all that at face value.

Soon, though, the real plan became clear. Kris was acting on my suggestion to form a "Mountaineer Fund," which I had envisioned as a way to pay some kids a few bucks to hand out literature door to door, make some phone calls, and encourage Republicans to get to the polls. Kris and Monty, though, apparently saw it as something else entirely—exactly what that was would only become clear over the course of the campaign. I knew the group would only be legal if it was working on behalf of all our candidates, and frankly, it was becoming more and more clear that the RNC's own field operation in West Virginia was going to fund and accomplish what should be the main goal of a group like this—getting out the vote.

But Kris and Monty began building the Mountaineer staff—all without my knowledge and without any input from me. I was beside myself as their behind the scenes machinations slowly became obvious. My first concern was that money that Kris would direct to the Mountaineer Fund to help Monty would detract from money which otherwise would come to us anyway; in other words, State Party contributions would be diverted into the Mountaineer Fund to benefit Monty.

Checks soon began arriving, often hand-delivered by one of the new "Mountaineer" staffers, made out to "West Virginia Republican Party—Mountaineer Fund." The understanding was that all of the activities of the Mountaineer group would be funded with money specifically earmarked for its efforts—no regular State Party money would be touched, Kris assured me.

That plan soon fell apart. The expenses and salaries of the Mountaineer group came due so soon that there was never even a chance to open a separate checking account for it. People were being hired, office space rented, computers and equipment leased, and even Monty Warner campaign signs and pamphlets being ordered, all at the expense of the West Virginia Republican Party. And the Chairman of the Party and his brother were orchestrating all of it with absolutely no consultation with the Party's Executive Director. Worst of all, everything I saw them doing seemed to be totally focused on one candidate.

I expressed my concerns several times to Kris, but he ignored my emails and conversations. As Executive Director, I was responsible for the day-to-day operation of the State Party. I was responsible for the money being spent, the activities of the staff, and trying to keep it all legal. And now this renegade group was operating out of a different headquarters virtually behind my back, in a conscious effort to circumvent any control by anyone except Kris and Monty.

The Mountaineer Fund quickly became a joke. Not nearly enough money came in to fund all the money being spent by the Mountaineers. The former phone vendor, who was now clearly in charge of the Mountaineers, began calling me on a regular basis begging me to pay salaries or expenses of Mountaineers from the State Party's regular account. I refused.

One morning as I was driving to work, the Mountaineer chief called me on my cell with an urgent request.

"Do you have a picture of Brent Benjamin?" he asked, referring to our Supreme Court candidate.

"I don't know. Why?" I replied.

"We have a mailer that needs to go to press in an hour, and we need Benjamin's photo," he said breathlessly.

"What kind of mailer?"

"A mailer with the whole ticket—Monty, Betty Ireland, Brent, all the state-wides, plus President Bush and Shelley Moore Capito."

I was livid.

"What?" I exclaimed. "Did you get all the candidates to sign off on this and approve it?"

He hesitated before answering, "Yes."

Monty had long been determined to present himself as the leader of a Republican Army of candidates, but had no regard as to whether the other candidates wanted to join his Army. I knew very well the Bush people would never OK such a mailer, and neither would Capito, but the guy responded to this question by affirming that everyone had signed off or was in the process of doing so.

I hung up and called Brent Benjamin.

"Do you know anything about a mailer going out from Monty's people with you and the other candidates on it?" I asked.

"No, I haven't heard a thing about it," he said. "And I don't want anything going out with me on it without my approval."

"Don't worry, it won't," I assured him.

I tracked down Betty Ireland, our Secretary of State candidate, and she also was completely in the dark about any mailer, and, like Brent, made me promise to stop it from happening.

I complained bitterly to Kris, but he waved off my concerns and excused the Mountaineers by claiming they were just over-anxious. What he seemed to ignore was the fact that it was completely illegal to feature both State candidates like Warner, Ireland and Benjamin, and Federal candidates like Bush and Capito, without following a complicated formula in regard to paying for it.

I was absolutely astounded that this flier was apparently an hour away from going to press, and the only thing that stopped what would have been a major disaster was the happenstance of a phone call from the Mountaineer leader to me trying to track down a photo. I stopped the mailer from happening, but the Mountaineer crew was not happy about it, which bothered me not at all.

For several days, I tried to focus Kris on how reckless this group was, how bad it would be for the Party's image in regard to what would once again be seen as Kris using the Party to help Monty with total disregard to the rest of the ticket, and the legal ramifications of various activities the Mountaineers were undertaking for which I could ultimately be held accountable.

The Mountaineer debacle was quickly spiraling out of control. The Mountaineer boss took an increasingly dismissive tone with me every time I questioned him on what he was doing. I talked with my wife, my parents, and a few close friends and associates, including Brent Benjamin and Rob Capehart (who was now serving as Brent's Campaign Manager in the Supreme Court race), about my deepening concerns. I could not continue to work at the Party under these circumstances. First, my Chairman had demonstrated a total disregard for my responsibilities and position, not to mention our relationship in regard to simple respect and trust. Secondly, I had no control at all on the activities of the Mountaineer group, but I could be held responsible for their actions.

I was on the verge of quitting, and Benjamin and Capehart offered me an escape route.

"If you need a place to land, you can work for my campaign," Brent said. "We'd love to have you. And we'd find a place for Ben and Olivia, too."

We discussed the ramifications my resignation would have on the Party, our candidates and our chances for victory in November. I had, through Kris' encouragement from the beginning, become pretty well known across the state as a principal voice of the Republican Party. Most people considered Kris and me inseparable politically, and thought of us as close friends, as well. My resignation would be a public sign of a major chasm, and lend credence to all those who were waiting for any excuse to pounce on the Warners.

That night, I discussed the issue at length with my wife. Lora was a West Virginia girl who I had met a couple of months after my arrival in Charleston. I had been divorced for eight years, and honestly believed I would never marry again. I was the father of four children—two grown into young adults, and two still in elementary school—and I had decided marriage was just not for me. Lora was much younger than me, but very mature and very sensible. The thing I loved about her most was that she never made mountains out of molehills. Throwing caution to the wind, we were married in March of 2002. It was one of my better decisions in life. She had always been politically active, and I could talk to her, knowing she understood the issues I was dealing with. She let me know she would stand beside me whatever I needed to do.

The next morning, I sent Kris a long email spelling out all my concerns, concluding that I regretfully could no longer work for the Party. It finally seemed to be the thing that got Kris' attention.

He came into the headquarters the next day, and we went to the private upstairs conference room to talk. He defended his actions by saying he was trying to spare me additional headaches and responsibilities by keeping me out of the Mountaineer group. I didn't buy that for a second. As far as I was concerned, he was simply proceeding behind my back with a plan devised by Monty and him because he knew how opposed to it I would be. I explained to him again how the setup and operation of the Mountaineer group was impossible and impractical.

"First of all," I said, "we shouldn't be hiring a staff like that until we have the money in place."

He shook his head. "You can't always wait for the money," he said, expressing a philosophy I knew he believed all too well.

Finally, after almost an hour, it seemed to become clear to him that I was serious about resigning. I knew he realized as well as anyone what a public relations disaster my resignation would be. Frankly, I wasn't interested in holding my resignation over his head. I truly wanted to just leave, then and there. Escaping from the growing nightmare of the Warner debacle in exchange for the exciting day-to-day adventure of the Benjamin campaign was appealing to me. But I didn't want to adopt a complete "my way or the highway" attitude, and I also didn't want to bring down our whole ticket by creating a public furor over the disarray of the State GOP.

"What is it you want to happen?" Kris finally asked.

"What I wish is that the Mountaineer group didn't even exist," I said, adding that at the very least, the former phone vender now running the group had to go.

"If he goes, will you run that staff?" Kris asked.

I thought about that for a long time.

"Yes," I finally replied, reluctantly. "But it has to be made clear that they exist not just for Monty, but for all of our candidates, and we have to bring all our candidates into the Mountaineer offices and make sure everyone knows that."

Soon, the Mountaineer boss was gone (or at least as far as I knew, although I still suspected over time that the Mountaineer staff was still in contact with him). I called Craig Bergman, who I knew from his computer work for us during the final weeks of the 2002 campaign, and arranged a meeting. I had always considered Craig a bit of a flake, frankly—he bounced from campaign to campaign, sometimes living in his van. His greatest allegiance and love seemed to be for Alan Keyes, who was embarking on yet another Don Quixote-esque battle in Illinois against Barack Obama for the U.S. Senate. Bergman told me he had actually been considering leaving West Virginia to work on the Keyes race, because, he said, Keyes was going to win.

I brushed off his prediction, because I felt Craig seldom had a good grasp on political reality. But he was talented on a computer, and good at compiling precinct walking lists for candidates. Craig seemed relieved that things were being worked out. He expressed his concerns that no one seemed to know who was in charge—the former Mountaineer leader had been constantly arguing with Monty's Campaign Manager, Dick Leggitt, over tactics and scheduling.

"From now on," I said, "no one at the State Party tries to tell the Warner campaign what to do. OK? And the Warner campaign does not tell us what to do."

Bergman quickly agreed. Now I needed to get a handle on all monetary commitments that had already been made.

"We've ordered 500 four-by-eight foot Warner for Governor signs," said Bergman.

"Paid for by the State Party?" I asked wide-eyed.

"Yep. Those were my instructions," he said.

"How much?"

"Uh, $11,000," he replied.

I shook my head. But it was too late to change it; the signs were being printed and would soon be delivered.

"All right," I said. "But nothing else for Monty Warner gets paid for by the State Party."

"I understand," said Bergman, adding sheepishly. "but we already have yard signs and bumper stickers, too. And the StatusquoJoe.com signs."
StatusquoJoe.com was a Web site someone on the Mountaineer side had devised to attack Joe Manchin, and hundreds of large, yellow, oversized signs had been ordered and paid for with State Party money to draw attention to the site.

"Is that it?" I asked.

"Uh huh," he nodded.

I took a deep breath. In all, Kris and Monty had already committed or spent around $20,000 in State Party funds—expenditures we could not afford—just for signs, bumper stickers and hand-outs. I thought about all those Republicans across the state who were worried that Monty's candidacy would mean the resources of the State Party would be focused solely on the Chairman's brother—and how right they were turning out to be.

13

Crunch time

While I was trying to reign in and reorganize the Mountaineer group, the Democrats around the state were doing everything they could to make it easier for us to elect Republicans to the Legislature.

Several headlines throughout the spring and summer reflected the ongoing scandals or questionable activities involving various Democrat officeholders.

"Director got free travel—Board member says Graham took trips to Hawaii, Disney"—*Charleston Daily Mail*, 3/26/04.

"Records connect Graham, Kiss"—*Charleston Daily Mail*, 4/21/04.

"Logan sheriff pleads guilty—Mendez resigns, will cooperate in vote-buying investigation"—*The Charleston Gazette*, 7/20/04.

"Ethics panel reopens Mezzatesta investigation"—*Charleston Daily Mail*, 8/6/04.

"Logan lawyer says he paid to buy votes—Mark Hrutkay says he is cooperating with U.S. Attorney in election fraud case"—*The Charleston Gazette*, 8/11/04.

"Mezzatesta inquiry taking toll on Hampshire County"—*The Charleston Gazette*, 8/15/04.

"Mezzatesta out as education chief"—*Beckley Register-Herald*, 8/17/04.

"Ethics panel to investigate Senator over Pete Dye vote"—*The Charleston Gazette*, 8/19/04.

"Legislators work under shadow of ethics scrutiny"—*The Charleston Gazette*, 8/24/04.

With the help of the Democrats in power, we had done a good job of creating the notion, justifiably so, that 70 years of unchallenged rule had led to an atmosphere of corruption and scandal in the State Legislature. With Republican candidates challenging every race, we were in a position to see significant changes on Election Day.

Our biggest obstacle to success, though, was not the Democrats, the media, or even the Bush campaign. Monty Warner's candidacy was quickly tearing the

Party apart. Ben Beakes came into my office almost daily to inform me of the calls of concern he was receiving on a regular basis from grassroots Republicans, County Chairs and candidates who were increasingly concerned or angry.

First, word was spreading that Kris was constantly making phone calls trying to raise money and build support for Monty, not for the Party. Secondly, activist Republicans and candidates felt Monty's message was not helping the ticket. Monty had decided to run on a theme of ending "cronyism and corruption" in West Virginia. Running against cronyism is a good message—unless your brother is the state GOP Chairman and your other brother is the United States Attorney for southern West Virginia. The hypocrisy of Monty's message was clear to everyone except the Warners.

Monty was pressuring candidates to make sure to run with him as a team and to promote his candidacy along with their own. But our House and Senate candidates were expressing growing concerns about linking their candidacies to his. Monty was clearly headed for a drubbing in November, and our candidates were much more interested in attaching themselves to President Bush, or even Brent Benjamin, than Monty Warner.

Kris, of course, was hearing none of this. He saw anyone's reluctance to team up with Monty as a sign of general Republican disloyalty. In fact, it was just the politics of reality. It wasn't that they disliked Monty—in most cases, they were still in his corner personally and wanted him to win—but the handwriting was on the wall early on regarding any chance he had in November.

Another source of embarrassment to the Warner campaign was a lack of public support from President Bush. During the President's many forays into the state, he at no point acknowledged Monty's existence. The closest the Bush campaign came to associating with the Warner campaign was on one occasion allowing Monty to be part of the pre-program at a Bush visit, with Monty speaking and back in his seat (and out of camera range) well before Bush was even onsite.

Even I sometimes thought the Bush campaign was going too far to distance itself from Monty. But any sympathy I would begin to feel for Monty would always be replaced by disbelief at the various antics he would pull.

Another nail in that coffin was driven hard in August. Jesse Jackson and Willie Nelson came to Charleston as part of their pro-labor, pro-Kerry tour. Television coverage and newspaper photos showed an unlikely ally holding hands with Jackson and company on stage—South Charleston Mayor Richie Robb.

Robb, of course, was a longtime Republican and candidate for Governor in the GOP Primary. And he was one of the five losing GOP gubernatorial candidates who Kris had named as Bush Electors for West Virginia. What was he doing with the Kerry crowd?

Soon, the local media was all over the story, and Richie caused a firestorm by refusing to commit himself to casting his Electoral vote for President Bush should Bush win West Virginia. The calls began pouring in from the RNC and the Bush campaign—why the hell did Kris Warner make Richie Robb a Bush Presidential Elector?

As one Bush campaign official told me later, "Frankly, we see this as just one more off-the-wall thing Kris did to help Monty." Indeed, Kris' motive in naming Robb and four of the other gubernatorial runners-up as Electors was a plan to appease them and get them on board with Monty.

What a nightmare this could be. If the 2004 Presidential race turned out to be as close as 2000, one renegade Electoral vote could once again make the election a circus act.

Publicly, our comment was that, in the end, we were sure Mayor Robb would do the "right thing." Privately, we didn't believe that for a second. RNC attorneys began looking closely at West Virginia law regarding Electors. In some states, Electors are legally bound to cast their votes for the winners of the popular vote. But not in West Virginia, and eventually the lawyers gave up and decided to wait until Election Day to determine whether any action would even be necessary. If Bush won enough states and enough Electoral votes, or lost by wide enough margins, Richie Robb's grandstand play would be irrelevant.

I was surprised Robb's possible defection did not become more of a national story than it did. West Virginia newspapers picked up on it, as well as local TV, but the only initial national attention came from CNBC, which sent in a reporter, and ABC, which asked some questions by phone but never followed up as far as I knew. Maybe they, too, decided that the story was only a story if the election results made it one.

Still, it cast a bad light on Kris, Monty, and the Party. I could not hold myself blameless, either. While I had indeed cautioned Kris not to name Electors without consulting the Bush campaign—advice he summarily ignored—I did not broach the subject with him again before he stood up at the State Convention and nominated his choices. I should have.

Like everyone else, I tried to just put the Richie Robb situation out of my mind. Like Scarlett O'Hara, I would think about it tomorrow, if necessary.

Monty and Kris were very different in some respects, but very similar in at least one area. Both were easily distracted by the latest bright idea or suggestion, and both had difficulty letting go of any perceived slight.

West Virginians for Life—the state's major pro-life organization—endorsed Joe Manchin for Governor not long after the Primary election. The endorsement was no surprise to me. I knew Manchin would gobble up nearly every important endorsement in the state, including those that would more typically go to a Republican. Manchin was viewed as a conservative, and he certainly had a pro-life voting record during his earlier tenure in the State Senate. Monty, of course, had no voting record at all, but was staunchly pro-life, and there was no doubt the abortion issue was more important to him personally than to Manchin. In its endorsement, the group made it clear that Monty was pro-life also, and they considered themselves winners regardless of who actually won the election.

As a Party, we spent a couple of days doing our duty and beating up on West Virginians for Life for their endorsement of Manchin, but I wanted to let it go quickly. Monty aside, the organization went on to endorse more Republican candidates in West Virginia than at any time in recent history. The Party could not ignore those endorsements by clobbering them constantly for failing to endorse Monty.

I'll never forget that much later, with just 35 days to go until Election Day, the Warner campaign called me with an idea they had conceived about a new way to punish West Virginians for Life. I had long forgotten about the issue, and all I could do was shake my head and advise them, "Let it go, guys." But it reminded me of what long and unforgiving memories they could have about any one or any group who was not on their team.

◆   ◆   ◆

The most beautiful time of year in the state of West Virginia is undoubtedly the Fall. The state is dominated by thousands of miles of foliage-covered mountain terrain, and when the leaves begin to change there is an explosion of bright red, orange and yellow that is indeed breathtaking.

This year, of course, the changing of the season was also ushering in the home stretch of the campaign. We had returned from the Republican National Convention in New York City surprisingly energized and refreshed. The West Virginia delegation had been treated very well, with all 30 of our Delegates seated front and center for the final night's address by the President. And the RNC had even given Monty about 60 seconds to take the podium during an afternoon session and make a couple of remarks.

It was telling, though, that when it came time to decide who would have the honor of ceremoniously announcing that West Virginia's delegates were cast for

President Bush, the Bush folks and the RNC demanded the honor go to Congresswoman Shelley Moore Capito rather than Monty, even though Shelley had graciously made it known she was happy to step aside. The last-minute edict caused a day-long stir among the Warners and the Bush folks. To me, it was another indication of the Bush campaign's true attitude toward Monty Warner.

Still, the Convention was an overall success for the West Virginia delegates and guests, and Ben and Olivia made the Party proud in their handling of most of the travel and sightseeing plans for our group. In fact, Kris and I had spent time in New York meeting and discussing a plan to keep the staff together after the 2004 election, with substantial raises for everyone.

"There's no reason to break up a winning team," he said.

I told him we could all think about it and talk again after Election Day.

But as the days of September quickly slipped by, our Party finances were beginning to look bleak. Kris was focused on raising money for Monty to the detriment of the Party he chaired.

On September 16, I sent Kris an email letting him know we needed him to do some serious fundraising in a hurry. But the very next morning, Kris informed me that he was going to be spending the day raising money for Monty. I asked him if he had seen my email about the Party's need for money. He said he had.

I was dumbfounded. While I knew very well—as did almost every Republican in the state—that Kris' attention had been almost entirely focused on Monty, he had never so blatantly admitted as much to me.

We were quickly going broke at just the time we should be ready to spend money on direct mail and phone programs for our House and Senate candidates, and while major donor fundraising was the one area the Chairman was uniquely responsible for, I was left with no choice but to do it myself. Providing any mail support or contributions for our candidates was at this point only a nice idea. Our immediate need was to raise money just to meet payroll and pay our utility bills.

I asked Olivia to compile a list of potential donors I could call, and I forwarded the list to Kris and asked if there was anyone I should not call for some reason. He wrote back and said no, call them all.

OK.

I started calling down the list, and within a couple of hours I had gotten pledges for about $10,000. The best selling point I had was the idea that we wanted to keep running a killer radio ad we were airing against Justice Warren McGraw, in our hopes of unseating him in favor of our own candidate, Brent Benjamin. The humorous ad, which I had scripted using taped outtakes of a wild, screaming, out-of-control tirade by McGraw at a Labor Day rally, had quickly become the talk of the political world in West Virginia. I did indeed intend to keep it running, so I could honestly make that pitch to our donors. (A later copycat version of this ad, funded by the Benjamin campaign, eventually won a national award for political advertisements.) For many donors, I had to quietly assure them their contributions would not go in any way to Monty Warner's campaign.

But I had only been in West Virginia for three years, and I did not have the longtime contacts or relationship with donors that Kris did. A couple of days later, Kris finally asked us to forward him some names he could call to raise money for the Party. I had by that time written and emailed him a four-page letter.

> *I believe that there is a general consensus among WV Republicans that Monty's campaign is just not gaining any traction, nor will it. There is also a general consensus that his candidacy was a bad idea to begin with—even among people who voted for him in the Primary. They believe that your attention as Chairman has been almost exclusively focused on Monty's campaign, both in fundraising and other support, at the expense of the Party...*
>
> *...The majority of our candidates see the Benjamin-McGraw race as the marquee race aside from Bush-Kerry. They also think Betty has a slim chance to beat Hechler. But they have pretty much written off Monty's race, and they are growing more and more uncomfortable with pressure to run as part of his "team."*
>
> *I have to say that I cannot imagine a scenario where Manchin loses. I don't think at this point an indictment, or a million dollar RGA campaign, or even catching Joe in bed with a dead hooker or a live boy would change the outcome.*
>
> *Chris Wakim (one of our House of Delegate incumbents running for reelection) says he was on a radio interview a couple of days ago, and as soon as he got off the air he got a call from Monty complaining that Chris had not mentioned or promoted Monty during the interview. I have no idea what Wakim really said in response, but he says that he finally told Monty that his race was going nowhere and he didn't need to be attached to it.*
>
> *We hear this all the time from our candidates—even the ones who personally like Monty but feel his campaign has gone nowhere and Manchin will win in a landslide, and they do not want their chances to be harmed by running as part of Monty's "team."*
>
> *...I know today you're trying to raise some money for us. But you have been stretched too thin. It was wrong for Monty to expect so much from you on his behalf—he should have realized you have a Party to run and could not devote so much time to his campaign.*

We have about 41 days to go and the staff here is devoted to seeing it through and doing everything in our power to win where we can. That is our focus, not this other speculation and complaining...

When Kris finally saw my letter about 24 hours after I sent it, he called to again defend himself and convince me how focused he had been all along on the Party and our House and Senate races. I was way beyond buying any of that, but I knew he had probably convinced himself of it. It was almost amusing to me that later that same day, he made two or three calls to me all on the subject of Monty and Manchin and what was happening in that race, as though our earlier conversation had never taken place. I understood well what others in the Party frequently told me happened when they tried to talk to Kris about how damaging Monty's candidacy was to the Party—he just wasn't getting it.

In the three years since Kris and I had been on board, we had never missed a payroll. That admirable record was now in serious jeopardy. On Monday, September 27, Kris—finally focused at least briefly on our desperate straits—traveled to Charleston to make fundraising calls from our headquarters.

"I'm going to stay here today, tomorrow, even Wednesday if that's what it takes until I raise about $20,000 to cover down on our immediate needs," he told me.

Kris had been able to pull off such fundraising feats in past months, but this time he found the going tougher. Vague promises of, "I'll see what I can do and get back to you," were about all he could accomplish. The landscape was very different with Kris' brother running for Governor, and I was convinced that donors who had been faithful in the past were now off the reservation, mostly because of Monty's candidacy.

It wasn't hard to understand this. Some of our biggest donors had been Monty's opponents in the GOP Primary, including: Dr. Doug McKinney, who usually maxed out to us every year, but was giving us nothing now; Dan Moore, the wealthy former banker and car dealer who had given us lots of money the year before; Senator Sarah Minear, a usually dependable large annual donor who had originally announced a run for Governor, then dropped out, then got upset over the handling of the vote for National Committee member, believing the Warners had ended up working against her; and many other donors who had supported other candidates in the Primary and now were punishing Kris for Monty's entry in the race and eventual Primary victory.

When Kris came to town, I suggested to him that we had to seriously consider disbanding or at least cutting back the Capitol Street gang, aka the Mountaineers.

"We're just overextended personnel wise," I said.

He shook his head. "These are the people who have established relationships with the precinct captains," he said. "There's just five weeks to go and I'm not going to cut them now."

Kris continued making call after call, meeting with little success. Payday was upon us, and we were short about $11,000, not to mention a payroll tax coming due within days totaling about $8,000.

Kris headed back to Morgantown, and soon after I emailed him this message:

> *If it appears that we cannot come up with the $8,000 to do the 941 payment and the $11,000 for the independent contract workers by tomorrow, I still have to come back to the idea of cutting at least some of the contractors...*
>
> *...Even if we can raise the money to pay them all, that's money that is taken away from what I'd rather be doing—direct mail for certain candidates in certain districts, not to mention some more direct contributions to some candidates.*
>
> *I think we need to take a hard look at at least cutting back the Capitol Street staff. We are obviously over-extended, and at this point unable to do anything in the way of House and Senate support, where we should right now be sending out mail going after Mezzestesta, Bailey, Ross, Plymale, etc.*
>
> *Please reconsider...talk to you soon.*

Within 10 minutes, Kris called and said, "Do what you have to do, man. I've never been so frustrated in my life trying to raise money."

Then he switched gears, and told me the Republican Governors Association had done a poll in the Manchin-Warner race and seemed to be encouraged.

"What were the results?" I asked.

"Well, they can't tell me the exact results, but they said this race is imminently winnable. All we have to do is raise some more money."

"Well," I said, chuckling out loud in spite of myself, "any race is imminently winnable if you raise enough money. The RGA is going to tell anyone that any race is imminently winnable if you raise the money."

"Yeah, that's true," he replied.

"And the thing to do," I continued, "is to let Dick Leggitt (Monty's campaign manager) and Monty raise their money, while you stay focused on raising money for the Party."

"Yep," he replied, unconvincingly.

The next day, Kris started the morning working the phones from his Morgantown office, and called me frequently with a recap of the contribution promises being proffered, which again were very much on the vague side. He said he would keep in touch.

A few hours went by and I heard no more from him, which I found strange after his initial flurry of morning calls. I called and left him a couple of messages that afternoon on his cell phone, but he didn't return my calls. Very odd.

It all became clear, though, when Dick Leggitt called me shortly after 5 p.m.

"What's up, Dick?" I asked.

"Oh, just fighting the brothers Warner," he said.

"Tell me what's happening."

"Well, Kris and Monty went down to see Buck Harless this afternoon trying to get some money for Monty," he said.

I quietly shook my head in amazement.

Dick went on to tell me that Buck told them he was going to do a poll, and if Monty was within 20 points, Buck would give some money.

Well, at least that was encouraging, I thought to myself, but not because Buck might give Monty some money. My reason for encouragement was that someone would finally do a poll on our side that offered a dose of reality and made Kris, if not Monty, realize what a futile effort Monty's candidacy was.

The only polling in the race from the Republican side had been the kind designed to give you the results you wanted, i.e., "If you knew Joe Manchin was Satan, and Monty Warner was the angel Gabriel, who would you vote for?" I was very curious to see a straight up, head to head legitimate poll, and maybe Buck would do one.

But this explained Kris' failure to return my calls all afternoon. He was back on the road trying to help Monty raise money while the State Party continued to sink.

In my heart, I sympathized with Kris. He did not want his brother to suffer the humiliation of a blowout. I had to believe that even Kris knew at this point that winning was out of the question, but saving face might be within reach.

What I could not get over was how Kris seemed unable to come to grips with the fact that every afternoon he spent helping Monty was an afternoon away from helping the Party he chose to chair. You cannot serve two masters, and truer words were never etched on biblical tablets. And I could not understand why this ex-Army Colonel, Monty Warner, at some point did not say, "Kris, your Party is in desperate trouble. You focus on the Party and I'll take care of my own campaign."

I had once so admired Kris for his drive and determination in the early days to fill the ballot and build a grassroots coalition. Now I wondered, was the reality closer to the fact that he was being driven behind the scenes all along by his brother, Monty, in preparation for a Monty Warner campaign for Governor?

The next morning, Kris called about some issue or the other, and never mentioned his visit to Harless. I wanted him to know that I was aware of his trip with Monty to see Harless, so before he hung up, I asked, "How's Buck?"

He hesitated for a moment before replying, "Buck's fine. He's going to do a poll for Monty. He loves the McGraw ad, and I told him anything he could do to help us keep it running would be helpful."

"That's nice," I said, letting it drop.

In frustration I began making another round of calls to some of the donors with whom I had built relationships. Plus, a friend from the Benjamin campaign gave me some new names to try, and I forwarded them to Kris and Olivia. A couple of them were friends of our great Raleigh County Chairman, Joe Long, and after Olivia called him, Joe suggested that I call one of the individuals because "Gary's personality will fit him better than Kris'."

I had managed to pay our main staff at headquarters, but checks for our Capitol Street staff, including the four I had let go, were now a day past due. I have always been a stickler for paying people, and paying them on time. There are others who disagree with this philosophy when crunched for money, especially in politics. Their attitude is that if people have to wait to get paid, that's a worthy trade-off if money needs to be put into advertising or mail or phone calls. I completely disagree. I think it sends a very bad message, i.e., our people are the least important items on our totem pole.

I think your people are your most valuable resource. Don't hire someone if you are not sure you will always be able to pay them, and pay them on time. I would let the electricity be turned off in the building if I had to make a choice between paying the light bill or paying an employee. Most people live paycheck to paycheck, and missing just one can result in dire consequences. They give you a good day's work every day, and in return, they deserve to be paid when they have been told they will be paid.

So it was very disturbing to me to miss a scheduled payday. That's why I was adamantly opposed to the hiring of the Capitol Street crew from the beginning—we had not raised the money first, and there was no guarantee of money coming in to pay them. But we were obligated to them now, and it was frustrating to me not to meet that obligation.

A day after I cut four of our Capitol Street workers, Tom Searls from *The Charleston Gazette* called and asked why we had closed our Martinsburg office (a Mountaineer outpost the Warners had established). Good news travels fast.

The spin I gave Tom was that with all the people the RNC and Bush campaign had hired in West Virginia, there was too much duplication of effort around the state. He seemed to accept it, and the next morning there was a short article buried inside the *Gazette*. Searls reported my explanation that the State GOP had laid off four field representatives "so the Party can spend more money in other areas, and to prevent duplication with the Republican National Committee and President Bush's re-election effort…"

Searls' article then shifted to the Monty Warner campaign, detailing a disputed bill the campaign had with a former mail vendor—a vendor we suspected had leaked both items to Searls.

The frustrating thing to me was not having the money to capitalize on some major opportunities that existed to go after the Democrats who were in the middle of scandals, many of which we helped to bring to light.

- An investigation had proven that a letter from House of Delegates member Jerry Mezzatesta had been created and backdated in an effort to mislead an ethics probe.

- Senator Billy Wayne Bailey was still receiving a salary from the Wyoming County Council on Aging while simultaneously directing Budget Digest money to that agency.

- Senator Mike Ross had voted for money to go to a golf course where he had a large personal financial interest.

- Multiple indictments had been handed down against various officials for activities related to vote-buying.

- House member Lidella Hrutkay's ex-husband Mark had been indicted for mail fraud in regard to vote-buying in his former wife's campaign.

- Gubernatorial candidate Joe Manchin was known to have used Mark Hrutkay's helicopter for travel in exchange for the use of Manchin's airplane, none of which was reported and was an apparent violation of campaign rules.

- House Speaker Bob Kiss served as legal counsel to the scandal-plagued Wyoming County Council on Aging and refused to discuss his work there. Kiss also had vigorously defended Jerry Mezzatesta prior to his investigation, and Kiss was known to be living in Charleston rather than in his district in Raleigh County.

- Justice Warren McGraw had blatantly flaunted ethics rules about judges staying out of politics by publicly endorsing Joe Manchin for Governor.

(McGraw had tried to tiptoe around the ethics rules by saying, "If I were going to do so, I'd be endorsing Joe Manchin for Governor of West Virginia.")

- McGraw's brother, Attorney General Darrell McGraw, had fired an office employee for ordering thousands of dollars of McGraw promotional items, despite the fact that McGraw's office had done exactly the same thing consistently over the years.

That was plenty of fodder for winning campaigns for our challengers, if we could only continue to get the word out. But it was October 1, and we were dead broke.

Despite our lack of money, I instructed Ben to proceed with putting together fliers and mailers to be sent from the State Party in the event that enough money came in to print and mail them. At least we would have them ready.

Out of curiosity, I decided to calculate just how much money we had spent on the Capitol Street/Mountaineer staff since Kris and Monty had quietly put it together back in June. When I was finished, I found that the amount we had paid already for the salaries, rent and expenses from June through September—four short months—had come to more than $93,000, and that didn't include expenses and Warner signs for which we still owed.

That was a staggering amount of money for a State Party with a full-year operating budget of $350,000—a budget which never had allowed for the formation of a separate staff and separate offices. In my mind, that was $93,000 that was spent on a staff and headquarters that was put together for the benefit of Monty Warner. That was $93,000 that we would have had when we needed it most for mail, phone and other candidate support. Instead of worrying about how we were going to make our third-quarter tax payment and meet payroll next week, we would have $93,000 in the bank. It literally took my breath away—and helped me realize that desperate times called for desperate measures.

14

The State Republican Party versus Kris Warner

With no money coming in the door and the Party Chairman focused almost entirely on his brother's race for Governor, I was ready to literally break ranks with Kris and begin operating independently of him.

My decision was reinforced several times in late September by calls and meetings with Ben and Olivia, both of whom were growing increasingly frustrated with Kris and were each strongly considering bolting the Party for more secure jobs and fewer sleepless nights. The conundrum reached the point where the only way I could keep them on board was to be frank with them, agreeing with their complaints about Kris and deciding on a course of action to go around him.

At this point, none of us were too concerned about Kris' reaction. We all felt he would be doing us a big favor by firing us on the spot. The only reason we were still there at all was to avoid a public embarrassment for Kris, the Party and our candidates.

So we jointly decided to shed our allegiance to Kris—we all felt he had shed his allegiance to us a long time ago—and start a new fundraising tact. Olivia began calling past donors who had dried up on us in the wake of the Warner debacle—people like Doug McKinney, Buck Harless and others who were angered over Monty's candidacy. We called these donors and let them know that we were well aware that Kris and Monty had put themselves ahead of the best interests of the Party. We answered honestly any questions they had about where our money had been spent, specifically letting them know about the $93,000 spent on Warner signs and the Capitol Street group.

Word quickly spread around the state that Kris had lost the loyalty of his staff, and phone calls began coming in from people who had spurned us for months, followed—after they were assured none of the money would go to the Warners in any way—by contributions coming in the mailbox. Additionally, I convinced our direct mail vendor to proceed with dropping a fundraising piece for us despite the fact we still owed them money from the last mailing we did.

We skimmed by day after day, with just enough money coming in to pay our core staff and keep the lights on and the doors open. The three remaining Capitol Street workers were not being paid, but I frankly was not as concerned about them as I was about our main staff at headquarters—the Capitol Street folks were there only because Monty and Kris had hired them in the first place behind my back, and the Warners could worry about them.

Then, on Saturday, October 16, I got a phone call from Brent Benjamin on my cell.

"Have you heard about the Bush-Warner signs?" he asked.

"What?"

"Yeah," said Brent. "I'm in the Eastern Panhandle, and I was just over at the Victory office. They tell me there are Bush-Warner yard signs out, and they say they're paid for by the State Party."

My blood boiled, and I replied, "If that's true, I will quit on the spot today." Kris had a couple of weeks earlier—desperate to somehow link the Warner campaign to President Bush, despite the efforts of the Bush campaign to distance Bush from Warner—asked my opinion of Monty doing Bush-Warner yard signs, and I told him there was no way to do it. First, the Bush people would never consent to it; secondly I knew of no way under campaign finance law to legally pay for a sign featuring both a federal and state candidate out of a state candidate fund—and I wasn't about to suggest the State Party pay for it.

Brent called back a few minutes later. He had tracked down one of the signs. They actually had a disclaimer, he said, that claimed they were paid for by something called the Northeast Conservative PAC, in small print below large letters that said "Bush, President, Warner, Governor."

While I was relieved that Kris Warner had not ordered Bush-Warner signs at the expense of the Party, I was still infuriated that he and Monty had obviously found a way to do what the Bush campaign had expressly forbidden them to do. I was tempted to contact someone on the Bush campaign, but I decided to wait for them to call me. First thing Monday morning, my phone rang with a call from Dave DenHerder, the Bush regional field rep.

Dave knew I had no part in the Bush-Warner signs, and was seeking my advice on how to deal with it.

"I see that President Bush has a new running mate," said Dave, struggling to make light of it.

"First of all, they're illegal," he continued. "Secondly, they're using the Bush logo without authorization." Indeed, when I finally saw one of the signs, it was obvious they had used the official Bush-Cheney yard sign and just replaced "Cheney" with "Warner."

Dave told me the Bush campaign was sending a cease and desist letter to the Warner campaign, and leaking it to the media as well. I fully agreed with both actions.

The Bush folks—never happy with the Warners from the beginning—were beside themselves. Later, Brian Donahue called to talk about the situation, and the next day Brent McGoldrick, the RNC Victory Director in West Virginia, came in to see me. Brent was working on putting together an election night celebration, which I had always anticipated would be one big event for Bush, Shelley Capito and all our state candidates. Brent's assignment now had become finding a way to hold the celebration, but exclude the Warner brothers.

Dick Leggitt, Monty's campaign manager, called me. He said he heard someone from the State Party was telling people they had to take the Bush-Warner signs down. I told him that was not true, but we were telling people we had nothing to do with them and were not distributing them. In fact, I had discovered the signs were being handed out from the Capitol Street Mountaineer office, and I had called and ordered staffers there to stop distributing them immediately and put them somewhere out of sight. I told Dick the Bush campaign was furious, and I was upset about it, too.

"Why are you upset?" he asked.

"Because it's just an unnecessary big middle finger to the Bush campaign," I replied.

"Listen, I've known Tom Josefiak for 30 years," said Leggitt, referring to the longtime Republican attorney who issued the cease and desist letter on behalf of the Bush campaign. "I called him, and he said the Bush campaign was sending thousands of these letters around the country. They're just protecting themselves. They're not upset at us."

"Well," I replied, "I can tell you that Dave DenHerder and Brian Donahue are upset."

"We had nothing to do with the signs," Leggitt protested. "An independent PAC did them."

I was insulted that Dick thought I was that naïve.

"Listen," I said. "I know who created the signs, and I'd be real careful if I were you telling people you had nothing to do with them."

In fact, purely by accident, Ben and Olivia had earlier discovered that the signs had been created on a computer at our Capitol Street office, and none of us believed for a minute that the sign was created without someone directing the designer to do so.

Dick paused. "Are you saying you're going to tell people who created them?" he asked, but then quickly added, "I had nothing to do with them."

By this time, I had not heard a word from Kris Warner for about five days. He was obviously aware by now that his staff had fully engaged in mutiny and, with just 13 days to go before Election Day, the best recourse was to try to ride it out. Every day, our phones rang off the hook with people from around the state asking for honest answers about what was going on with the Warners. And we gave them honest answers.

By October 22, Scott Saxton of WSAZ-TV, had discovered and reported on a link between the Northeast Conservative PAC and the Warner campaign. A Warner campaign staffer shared the same D.C. address as the PAC. The Manchin campaign held an afternoon press conference to pile on, and calls began coming into our headquarters from Republicans poised and ready to dump Kris immediately. They were angry that not only was the Warner campaign becoming an embarrassment to Republicans in general, but it had also completely alienated the Bush campaign.

Despite the cease and desist letters, Kris and one of his other brothers were seen personally putting up the Bush-Warner signs all across West Virginia. The Democrats held a press conference and unveiled a photo of Bush-Warner signs piled into the back of Monty Warner's own truck. The whole thing was beyond belief.

I still believed that the interests of the Party would be served best by getting through the election—now just 11 days away—before trying to act on the Warner problem. But holding off the angry mob was no easy task. Monty Warner's campaign by the end had quickly deteriorated into the stereotypical last acts of a desperate candidate. In the waning days of the campaign, Monty accused Joe Manchin of being AWOL during the Vietnam War. Kris accused Manchin of lying about receiving a football scholarship to West Virginia University. And before their final debate, someone outside the debate site was actually seen distributing fliers referring to a completely unsubstantiated rumor regarding Manchin and an alleged extramarital affair.

I am all for hardball politics, but accusations must have some truth to them somewhere. No one gives credibility to charges that only emerge in the final days of a campaign from a candidate losing by 30 points.

The final insult for the Warners came from the Bush campaign and the RNC. Brent McGoldrick called me on the Thursday before the election and told me officially that the Bush campaign, the RNC and the Capito organization had all decided they did not want the Warners attending the big Election Night celebration being sponsored by the RNC at the Embassy Suites hotel in Charleston. The State Party staff and our candidates were welcome, but the Warners were not. Brent asked me to make the call and let the Warners know.

Normally, a major Party gubernatorial candidate would be holding his own separate election night event, just as Joe Manchin was planning to do. But I knew Monty had no such plans, probably in part because he knew how badly he was going to lose and knew how small his crowd of supporters would be, and in part because he had no money.

"How do you think they'll react?" Brent asked me.

"I think they'll be pissed, and they'll show up anyway," I replied.

I could have told Brent he needed to make the call himself. But over the course of three years, I had been the go-between for Kris Warner and the RNC/ Bush folks on countless subjects. When Kris wanted something from the RNC that we both knew the RNC wouldn't want to do, it was my job to ask. When the RNC had bad news for Kris, I was the one asked to deliver it. I considered it part of my job, and I wasn't going to make some excuse now not to do it, particularly when I shared the RNC's sentiments on the subject.

I called Dick Leggitt, Monty's campaign manager, and informed him of the RNC message.

"F**k the RNC," said Leggitt. "I've been doing this for 30 years. This is a Victory 2004 event, and it's paid for by Victory donors from West Virginia. You tell them we'll be there anyway."

Pretty much what I expected to hear. Dick Leggitt was, indeed, a longtime veteran of Republican hardball politics. I personally liked Dick, and we had several lunch meetings throughout the campaign commiserating about trying to work for the Warners. But Dick was also a pro hired to do a job, and he was dedicated to doing everything he could for his candidate.

I knew Leggitt would be on the phone to Kris right away, but I dialed Kris' cell phone anyway. I got his voicemail, and left a message detailing the RNC's wishes. It wasn't until the next morning that I heard back from Kris.

"As long as you're delivering messages," he said sarcastically, "tell the RNC that the last time I checked I'm still the top-ranking RNC member in West Virginia. If they want to tell the state Chairman he can't attend their Victory event, someone from the RNC needs to pick up the phone and tell me himself."

In the meantime, I heard that Leggitt had emailed Coddy Johnson at the Bush campaign and threatened to call a press conference blasting the RNC and Bush campaign for keeping the Warners out of their Victory celebration. Leggitt no doubt felt he would frighten the Bush folks by convincing them that Monty's supporters would be so outraged that it could hurt Bush at the polls on Election Day. My personal feeling was that Monty had so few supporters it wouldn't matter, and anyway, Monty's supporters were Bush supporters first. But the RNC and Bush folks got cold feet and wanted to avoid any distractions going into the election, so they backed off. Instead of banning the Warners, we agreed to set aside a separate, smaller room just for Monty and the State Party candidates so Monty could not share the same stage with Shelley Moore Capito and the Bush celebration. Once again, the RNC and Bush campaign's antipathy toward Monty would cause all of our candidates to pay a price.

15

Someone's gotta go, so I guess it'll be me

Election Day finally arrived. The past two years had been the most exhausting of my life. The emotional toll of playing go-between and peacemaker with the Warners, the Bush campaign and the RNC—not to mention all of our state House and Senate candidates, County Chairs, Executive Committee members and donors—was a heavy one. But the magic day had finally arrived, and some kind of end was in sight.

On Election Day, Kris Warner delivered the cruelest cut of all to his long-suffering staff. On a day when even all the turmoil of the past months could not dampen the staff's enthusiasm for the possibilities that awaited us within the election results, Kris found another way to kill our spirits. He showed up at the headquarters for the first time in weeks, and met with each staff member one-on-one, delivering the same message, starting with me.

Kris said that obviously the situation with the staff was not working out. He suggested that the whole staff take two weeks unpaid vacation, then reconvene to let him know what our future plans were. In politics, the end of an election cycle is not a time for unpaid time off. In fact, it's a time when you can usually count on bonuses and a lot of earned vacation time. This year, our reward was to take time off without pay.

I let Kris know that none of us were in a position to take any unpaid leave. OK, he said. In that case, then, he would be back in Charleston on Friday, and he needed our decisions then. Also, he said, he wanted to be the one talking to the press that night as results came in. He said he did not want me doing any media interviews. He wanted me to direct them all to him.

After delivering the Friday ultimatum to the rest of the staff individually, Kris left the building. One by one, the staff gathered in my office. We just looked at each other and shook our heads. I told them to get through the evening, and we would discuss the issue on Wednesday.

The staff and I headed to the Embassy Suites to oversee the set up for the small side room which our candidates would now be using. Meanwhile, I heard that the radio network where Hoppy Kercheval worked, MetroNews, was doing exit polling on the presidential and gubernatorial races. I called Hoppy to see if he would share the mid-day results. Hoppy told me that Bush was leading Kerry by nine or 10 points, and Manchin was blowing out Warner, 66 percent to 33 percent. In fact, Hoppy said, MetroNews was planning to call the race for Manchin about five minutes after the polls closed at 7:30.

I thought about keeping the results to myself—Kris might think I was just rubbing it in if I called to share the bad news—but then I decided that Kris should know the numbers and MetroNews' plans for an early call just in case Monty wanted to plan for an early concession speech. I called Kris and gave him the numbers Hoppy had given me. He thanked me, but made no further comment.

Some of the TV reporters were already gathering at the Embassy Suites to do live shots on the 6 p.m. news. They asked if I would interview with them. Despite Kris' instructions, I said sure. Kris was nowhere around, and I was determined to do my job until it was my job no longer.

In fact, I did many TV, radio and print interviews that night. By 8 p.m., with the polls closed and the race already called for Manchin, the press kept asking me when Monty Warner was going to show up and concede. I called Kris repeatedly but could not reach him. He was not returning my voicemails. Finally, a reporter told me he had reached Dick Leggitt, and Leggitt said Monty would not be coming over until they saw the actual results from 16 counties they were tracking. Leggitt said the exit polls were wrong.

Reporters were going on air live throughout the evening and subtly ridiculing Monty for failing to show up. Manchin went ahead with his victory speech from his Morgantown headquarters, without the courtesy of a Monty Warner concession. Finally, around 10 p.m., Monty showed up, with Kris at his side.

Aside from the Governor's race, the Election Night of Nov. 2, 2004, turned out to be a historic one for West Virginia Republicans, but not as historic as it should have been. President Bush won the state by more than 13 points. Shelley Moore Capito won reelection by 16 points. Republican Brent Benjamin, thanks in large part to our radio ad featuring an out of control Warren McGraw and to a million-dollar independent 527 effort led by Massey Energy's Don Blankenship, won a seat on the Supreme Court by four points, tipping the balance of the

Court from pro-labor to pro-business. Republican Betty Ireland won a two-point victory for Secretary of State over well-financed and well-known Ken Hechler.

In the State Legislature, we defended every one of our incumbent seats, picked up three more seats in the State Senate (including beating the "unbeatable" Mike Ross), and netted one pickup in the House of Delegates, including a victory over Jerry Mezzatesta. While we should have done better in the House, the fact is we started the night down by four seats, with one retirement, two House members running for the Senate, and one House member, Larry Faircloth, running for Governor. In essence, we had to win five additional seats to have a net gain of one. Not bad.

But it should have been much better, and I will always be convinced that if the focus of our state Chairman and our Party resources had not been so devoted to Monty Warner's race, we would have won countless more state House and Senate races.

Kris left the Election Night party not long after Monty's concession speech. He was not there for Betty Ireland's victory speech, or Brent Benjamin's appearance. Ben Beakes and I went to Party headquarters around 2 a.m. and tracked the progress of a couple of tight Senate races until around 6 a.m.

Just a few hours later, I held a meeting with my staff. We gathered upstairs in the same conference room where Kris and I had been threatened by Monty just after the Primary that he would "pull the rug out" from under us. It was the same room where Kris and I had met in early August when I was on the brink of resigning over the Mountaineer group. Now, the six of us on headquarters' staff—Ben, Olivia, Stephanie, and field reps Mik Carpenter and Jenny Babcanak—gathered for what we knew might be our final meeting as a group.

"I've been in management for 20 years," I told them. "I'm not a fan of employee revolts. But I think it's clear we're all in agreement on this issue."

They all nodded their heads, and Ben spoke up.

"Gary, whatever you do, we're with you," he said. That meant a lot to me, and I thanked them for their hard work and loyalty to the Republican cause.

On Thursday, two members of the Republican State Executive Committee, Jim Reed and Don Nickerson, traveled to Morgantown to meet with Kris Warner and ask him to consider resigning. They were Committee members who had long been among Kris' most ardent supporters. They met with Kris for more than four hours, but in the end, he wouldn't budge.

I told my staff to stay out of the office on Friday, that I would meet with Kris alone, and then I would call them to let them know what happened. In the meantime, some Committee members suggested that if Kris honestly wanted what was best for the Party, he might agree to resign and name me interim Chairman until a permanent Chair was elected by the Committee. I prepared a resignation letter to that effect, but kept it in my drawer to be used only if Kris gave any indication he might consider such a move—which I did not think he would do.

Knowing Kris was on his way to Charleston to meet with me, Jim Reed and our newly elected Supreme Court member, Brent Benjamin, came to the office and were there when Kris arrived. I noticed that when Kris came in, he had with him two people from Monty's campaign, who waited in an outer office.

Brent and Jim again urged Kris to resign. We all three promised to send him out on a high note, with praise for everything he had done for the Party. In fact, on the slight chance he might resign, I had already written a press release giving Kris credit for almost every good thing under the sun. Kris waited until we were finished.

"Anything else?" he asked.

Everyone shook their heads. Jim Reed, totally frustrated by this time, got up and left the building. Kris asked Brent to leave as well so he could speak with me alone, but I told him I wanted Brent to stay. I wanted a witness to whatever Kris was going to do or say.

"OK," Kris said with a shrug. He reached into his pocket and handed me a letter. I opened it, and read my termination notice. The letter gave no reason for the termination, but ordered that I was to be out of the office that day. I got up from my desk, and asked if I could return later to get my things, to which he agreed.

After I left, Kris called Ben Beakes, and Ben in no uncertain terms informed Kris of a particular anal cavity where he could deposit his job. In fact, the whole staff quit when they learned of my termination. The front page headline on a story by Tom Searls in the next day's *Charleston Gazette* summed it all up: "GOP's Kris Warner axes Party's W.Va. Executive Director—'staff change' comes after Party makes historic gains in state."

Searls wrote that I was fired and the other staff members quit "just three days after the election" in which "the Party picked up one House seat, where it now will trail Democrats 67-33, and three Senate seats, where it now has 13 of 34 seats. The state GOP also captured two statewide races, winning a state Supreme Court seat and the Secretary of State's office."

Searls' article reported on the speculation that Kris had lost much of his support on the State Executive Committee because he spent so much time on Monty's gubernatorial campaign, rather than trying to help other candidates.

The story also quoted a couple of Republicans, including state Young Republican Chairman Charles Bolen, who said the staff had done outstanding work, and added, "I don't like the idea of staff being fired after the most successful election in 70 years."

For his part, Kris was quoted as claiming the firing was just part of a "staff change," and shrugged it off. Once again, he was tragically miscalculating public perception and failing to recognize the consequences of his own actions.

Even though I knew either Kris Warner or the staff had to go, Kris' firing of me still left me shaken. I guess deep down I thought Kris would not sacrifice a great staff that obviously had been effective, in exchange for his own weakened survival. He truly had a one-time chance to announce his resignation and paint it as a Chairman going out on top, all things considered. But his ego would not let that happen, and he chose to set the stage for months of drawn out controversy and negative publicity, affecting all Republicans in the state.

I spent the afternoon calling my wife, other family members, friends and various Republican officials. One of the hardest calls I made was to my young son, Jonathan, who Kris had taken hunting on that cold Saturday afternoon a couple of years before. Jonathan felt he had gotten to know Kris pretty well that day, appreciated Kris' gesture in going out of his way for us, and thought Kris and his dad were pretty good friends.

"Why would Kris fire you?" he asked. I didn't know how to explain the reality of politics to him in a way he could understand at that young age.

"Oh, I don't know," was about all I could muster. "Just the way it is sometimes in politics. Don't worry."

That same afternoon, Ben and Olivia returned to the headquarters to get their personal belongings, and Scott Saxton of Channel 3 brought news cameras to record the event. The cameras caught a glimpse through the window of Jack Rohrer, a Monty Warner for Governor worker who Kris would soon name the Party's acting Executive Director, inside the headquarters locking the door behind him. Later, another one of Kris and Monty's Mountaineer employees posted an online diary describing the incident from his point of view inside the building.

> *Gary didn't go quietly. He, Ben and Olivia all went straight to the newspapers, talk shows, and even TV to spread the mess on their way out. When Ben and Olivia returned to get their personal belongings, they even brought media cameras to record a speculated confrontation. We headed them off at the pass—I was in the midst of looting Ben's office for cool pens and checking his computer for files when my cell phone buzzed: Craig. "DUDE THEY'RE HERE AND THEY BROUGHT MEDIA CAMERAS WITH THEM! Get upstairs before they see you!!" I punched the monitor off and hauled out of the office and up the stairs,*

ducking under the windows and rolling across the floor into the conference room, laughing and giggling like a complete dork. Jack, Craig and I peeked out the windows to see Channel 3 pointing their camera at the front door. "THAT'S a good one!" I said, still laughing. "Live footage of a deserted building. Whoopdie freakin' doo, that'll make the 7:00 news I tellya!" Jack eventually chased the cameras away before letting the kids in to gather their stuff. I wanted to see Ben so I could laugh in his face...they wouldn't let me. That idiot figured us for dim light bulbs and assumed he could get the media to catch us in a confrontation—an absurd idea in the first place, and all the more pathetic that he wasn't mature enough to resign gracefully.

(Months later, when Scott Saxton got hold of the diary entry, he again ran the footage he had collected that day, this time adding the diary description of events, with video of poor Olivia crying while rummaging through the dumpster where Kris' new crew had tossed some of her belongings.)

That evening, I stopped in at a reception being held downtown for Brent Benjamin. Betty Ireland, our newly-elected Secretary of State, was there, and when she saw me, she gave me a hug and said, "That sonuvabitch."

I just shook my head.

"Gary, I can offer you a job as my Chief of Staff," she said, "I know it doesn't pay what you need to be making. But it's yours if you want it."

She was right about the pay range, but her gesture meant more to me at that moment than she could know. I thanked her, and we discussed the fact that her Chief of Staff position would actually be an ideal fit for Ben Beakes, and Ben was offered and accepted the job a few days later.

Over the next few days, I kept in touch with Olivia and Stephanie, and through Ben kept tabs on our two other staffers, Mik and Jenny. None of them would have much difficulty finding employment, but in the short term I knew they would be struggling. I wanted to make sure they knew they could count on my help in any way. Their loyalty in sticking by me was something I would never forget, even though I knew that more than sticking by me, they were sticking by their principles. They had all bought into the vision Kris had originally painted—that winning the State Legislature was our goal above all else. Kris' actions during the course of the campaign had disillusioned us all, and like me, none of them could work for him any longer.

The next few days were a strange blur. I did countless media interviews. The Bush folks were great—they quickly let me know that if I wanted it, a Federal job awaited me in the Administration, and in the meantime they offered me a job immediately with the Presidential Inaugural Committee, making the same offer to Ben and Olivia. Legislators, Committee members and grassroots supporters contacted me to share their shock and disappointment. Many of them offered help with finding a job if I needed it, but I had been around long enough to know that while their intentions were good, most of them weren't in a position to offer me something that was a good fit for my experience and salary needs.

The only concrete job possibility from within West Virginia offering the kind of money I had been making in recent years came from Brent Benjamin. While most of the jobs in the state Supreme Court were for law clerks, requiring a legal degree, Brent also would need to hire an Administrative Assistant—primarily a secretarial position, but one that paid nearly as much as I had been making at the State Party. Brent talked about making the job more than secretarial in nature, and it would offer great state health insurance benefits and a less hectic and more stable life. Brent, though, was still somewhat fixated on the idea of me returning to the State Party if Kris would make a relatively quick exit. I knew that was unlikely—Kris would dig in for a long fight rather than ever admit defeat—and frankly, a more dependable, less political job at this point was very appealing to me. In fact, after discussing it with Brent during a subsequent one-day trip to Washington we took together, I sent him a letter, formally applying for the position and summing up why it was so appealing to me.

In my public comments, I did my best to contain any anger at Kris in favor of a *c'est la vie* attitude, with varying degrees of success. For his part, while Kris started out claiming the move was just a "staff change," it wasn't long before he was insinuating it was my fault for not winning more House seats.

As the days rolled by, I heard from many reporters that Kris was growing increasingly irritated by the fact this story would not go away. At one point, a TV reporter told me Kris barked at him, saying, "Why is this still a story? You couldn't even tell me who the Executive Director was in most states!" What Kris failed to realize was that I was the alter ego he had created. Kris had originally hired me for my communication background. He wanted me to, at the very least, share the stage with him as the public face of the Party. And when we were in hot water on something, he wanted me to be the primary face of the Party. Now, he wanted to turn that off like a light switch, but in reality my firing had the exact opposite result.

On Sunday, November 7, The Associated Press moved a story headlined "Republican officeholders question Party official's firing," and quoted several state House and Senate members upset with Kris' actions. Delegate Ray Canterbury insisted that Kris needed to answer some "serious questions." Delegate Linda Sumner said she wanted to hear some reasons for the firing. Senator Steve

Harrison said the staff had been doing a good job, and our election successes made the turn of events even more puzzling. Supreme Court Justice-elect Brent Benjamin issued a statement that he was "deeply saddened" by the firing and staff walkout. And Senator Donna Boley, never a fan of Kris', called for an investigation.

Many other stories appeared, speculating on special meetings of the Executive Committee being called, Kris being asked to resign, and totaling up how much Party money had been spent on the Monty Warner campaign. I knew the media frenzy was not what Kris thought would result from his actions. As they say in the business, this story had legs.

16

Do not go gentle into that good night

While the turmoil over the brothers Warner continued to grow, I needed to decide whether to actively seek other employment, or wait to see if members of the state GOP Executive Committee could organize themselves well enough to act on the State Party situation and possibly land back there myself, either resuming my Executive Director role or even becoming Chairman, an idea floated by several Committee members. There was a big part of me that was not ready to leave the Party—I felt our mission was only half accomplished.

In the meantime, I took up the Bush folks and the RNC on their offer to help me buy some time by joining the Presidential Inaugural Committee in Washington. It would be exciting to be part of President Bush's Inauguration, and it would provide me with a few paydays during December and January. The position would require me to live in Washington for a couple of months, and the generosity of my old friend and former Ohio Party boss, Tom Whatman, made that part of the equation easy enough. As part of his consulting business, Tom maintained a small apartment in Washington, but spent only a week or so there each month. Tom readily agreed to let me crash at his D.C. apartment while I worked with the Inaugural Committee.

In mid December, a bombshell was dropped, with the former Warner for Governor Campaign Manager, Dick Leggitt—who had not been paid in weeks by Monty Warner—going public about the real source of the Bush-Warner signs. Soon thereafter, *The Charleston Gazette* ran a front page headline, "Kris Warner got yard sign e-mail—state Chairman denies involvement with Bush-Warner placards."

Gazette reporter Scott Finn reported that, several days before the appearance of the signs, Kris had actually received an email from one of his contract employees that included the design for the sign. After weeks of absolute denials by Kris that he had any connection with the signs at all, someone in Kris' office had forwarded the email to Finn, and it clearly showed that Kris was well aware of the development of the signs.

Dick Leggitt had had enough of not getting paid and reading outright lies in the papers. He came out in the media claiming in detail that the Bush-Warner signs were ordered by Kris, paid for by Kris, and deployed at Kris' directions. Kris, of course, denied everything, even in the face of overwhelming evidence.

Leggitt, in fact, claimed that Kris paid for part of the signs with what he described as a bogus expense check from the Monty Warner for Governor account. Leggitt said Kris had instructed the check be made out for an odd amount to avoid scrutiny. Kris then had endorsed the check directly to the Washington-based PAC whose disclaimer appeared on the signs.

Kris initially denied to Finn that he had signed the check over to the PAC, but Finn had actually obtained a copy of the check demonstrating that very fact, and Kris had to own up to it, saying he had "forgotten" signing the check over.

I had departed for Washington to work on the Inaugural Committee in early December, but back in West Virginia, several Executive Committee members were putting plans into motion to depose Kris Warner. Led by National Committeeman and Committeewoman Jim Reed and Donna Gosney, as well as a Party Vice Chairman, Bob Fish, an ad-hoc "Split Rail Committee" was formed. Fish invited me to attend their initial meeting on a Saturday, and I flew back from D.C. to join them.

About 10 members of the "Split Rail Committee" showed up at the offices of Jim Reed in Charleston. The full Executive Committee meeting was only three weeks away. I helped craft a letter to be sent to the full Committee, detailing the allegations of the former Warner for Governor Campaign Manager, Dick Leggitt, as well as an explanation of the amount of State Party money that had been allocated for the Warner campaign. Committee members were asked to unofficially vote a "confidence" or "no confidence" ballot on Kris Warner and return them to Fish.

I returned to Washington, but for several days, and despite my earlier pledge, I spent as much time doing radio and newspaper interviews by phone with West Virginia media as I did working on the Inauguration. Meanwhile, Fish, Reed, Gosney and company were formulating a plan for the meeting of the full Committee. They decided that Reed would, at some point, call for a no confidence vote on Kris, and they met with the Rules Committee to come up with somewhat of a "trial" format in which those opposed and those supportive of Kris would have equal time to make their case.

Several Committee members arranged for me to carry a proxy to the meeting so I would be guaranteed the right to speak. When the day arrived, I flew into Charleston, and then my wife and I made the 70-mile drive to Flatwoods, where the meeting was being held.

The Day's Inn was packed for the meeting. Kris, in an effort to focus Committee members on our successful candidates rather than on his actions as Chairman, had made sure to invite nearly every candidate or officeholder to attend. Many of them were there, including state GOP House and Senate leaders Charles Trump and Vic Sprouse, respectively, as well as our new Secretary of State-elect, Betty Ireland. Reporters were on hand as well, including several TV cameras.

I had warned members of the "Split Rail Committee" that Kris Warner was a master of avoidance and delay. Since this meeting was officially the regular winter meeting, Kris had front-loaded the agenda with regular Party business—a long series of reports, remarks from candidates and officeholders, etc.—with "new business" falling last, of course, on the agenda.

Betty Ireland spoke early in the meeting, and after discussing her campaign and her plans for the Secretary of State's office, she took Kris by surprise by calling for "new leadership" for the State Party. Kris dropped his head and frowned, apparently thinking Betty was going to be supportive of him.

Shortly thereafter, Jim Reed stood and asked to be recognized, and said, "It is with a heavy heart that I call for a no confidence vote on the Chairman."

Hiram Lewis, who had been our candidate for Attorney General and was now serving as Kris' hand-picked choice for Party Treasurer, was obviously prepared for Reed's motion, and Lewis took the microphone to argue that the motion was out of order. Fish, an expert parliamentarian, argued correctly that Lewis was wrong, but what ensued was the kind of confusion that Kris Warner was clearly striving to achieve. In the end, the Committee voted to delay the no confidence vote until the end of the meeting. I knew then that the effort to topple him was in trouble.

Meetings of the West Virginia Republican State Executive Committee were always lengthy and boring. They typically lasted three or four hours, and by their conclusion everyone was always more than ready to hit the road in a hurry, especially Committee members who had driven several hours across the state to attend. On this day, when the time for new business finally arrived—a good three hours after the meeting had begun—everyone agreed to take a 10-minute break to stretch their legs.

When the Committee came back into session, Bob Fish approached the microphone. Everyone was prepared to address the issue we had all been waiting for.

"Mr. Chairman," said Fish. "In the interest of Party unity, I move that we adjourn."

I sat stunned in my chair, as did most of the other Committee members. The pro-Warner faction quickly seconded Fish's motion, and fled the premises. I looked at Jim Reed, and Donna Gosney, and shook my head, finally making my way to the exit.

"What happened?" I was asked over and over again by Committee members on my way out the door. I had no answers for them.

Bob Fish left a message for me the next day, asking for my take on the meeting, but I was too angry to call him back for a few days. In the meantime, I had learned that some of our legislative leaders had convinced Bob during the 10-minute break that the votes might not be there, and a public war on Kris would be bad for the Party. They begged him to let it drop, promising to deal with it later in a less public fashion.

While Kris Warner had managed to avoid facing a vote on his Chairmanship, he had, in reality, emerged from the Committee meeting the lamest of ducks. His ability to raise money for the Party was nil, and within days rumors began spreading that he had met with Republican "leaders" and let them know he would be willing to resign his Chairmanship, on the condition that the Party's $100,000 debt be erased first. As time went on, various GOP leaders who talked to Kris seemed to come away consistently believing the Chairman was about to resign at any time, failing to understand that this was how Kris continued to buy time until he figured out something else.

By this time, though, it was quickly becoming academic to me. While I still could not honestly deny an interest in returning to the Party if Kris would step down immediately, I had to begin seriously exploring other opportunities. By mid-January, my work with the Inaugural Committee was winding down, and all of us working there were promised jobs with the Bush administration—but those jobs would require working in D.C., which, because of the distance from my children in Ohio, was an impractical choice for me.

I was still heartened by the possibility of the job with our new Supreme Court Justice, Brent Benjamin. Of all the Republicans who had assured me of a "safety net" while I was putting my job on the line with the West Virginia Republican Party, Brent was the one I felt would be the most likely to come through.

In late January, after my Presidential Inaugural Committee responsibilities had ended and I had returned to Charleston, I called Brent, and we met at a downtown coffee shop. After some small talk about the latest rumors swirling around the Warners, Brent finally came to the subject at hand.

"In regard to the job as my Administrative Assistant," he began, "I talked it over with some folks, and basically it is just a secretarial job, and I had to fill that two weeks ago."

I'm sure my face turned three shades of red.

Brent went on, talking about some other job opportunities he thought might be available, but frankly, I wasn't hearing a word he said. After a few more seconds, I reached for my coat.

"I have to go," I said. He walked out to the sidewalk with me, but I was angry, and I was hurt, and I quickly said my goodbyes.

Part of me could understand Brent's reluctance to hire me. He was embarking on a job as a member of the West Virginia Supreme Court. He was already under constant accusations that his election was due to the partisan influence and money of Don Blankenship, the Massey Energy coal boss who had personally spent more than $2 million in anti-McGraw advertising. The last thing Brent needed was the publicity of hiring a well-known partisan Republican as a top assistant, opening the door to even further accusations that the Court would be hopelessly politicized.

Brent and I had become close friends, and I had personally made sure the State Party spent what little money was available, after the funds wasted on Monty's race, on our effective multi-week radio campaign for Brent. I felt Brent could have at least taken me on board until the possibility emerged for me to return to the Party. But it was an emotional time for me, and I liked Brent too much to hold it against him forever. He was under his own set of pressures, and eventually we would resume our friendship.

◆   ◆   ◆

Ever since Kris had fired me, I had, of course, been in contact with my Ohio friends, including Tom Whatman and Jim Nathanson—the same Jim Nathanson who had, more than three years before, gently warned me about stepping into the landmine of West Virginia politics. Jim lived in Dayton, and in addition to his state and national work, was heavily involved in Montgomery County, Ohio, politics. A good friend of his was a longtime Montgomery County Commissioner, who was looking for a new chief assistant.

Tom suggested to Jim that I might be interested. Indeed, the job was appealing on a number of levels. The salary was not what I could make if I was willing to work in D.C. or other places outside further from my kids, but it was in line with what I had been making at the Party in West Virginia, plus the county government benefits were excellent. I had some discussions as well with friends who were building staffs for the various GOP candidates in the important Ohio gubernatorial races pending in 2006, but jumping into high-profile campaign mode was not something I was eager for on the heals of the nightmare from which I had just emerged.

Montgomery County's population exceeded a half million people, making this one county alone more than one-fourth the size of the whole state of West Virginia. The County Commission in a county like Montgomery was an important entity. I would be living less than an hour from my children, and for a while at least, the job would offer more of an 8 to 5 lifestyle rather than the 24/7 aggravation of campaign politics. Eventually, after interviewing with the Commissioner, talking with my wife and deciding that relocating to Ohio was an acceptable decision to all, I accepted the job.

At around the same time, Olivia Kelley, the Party's former Finance Director, was offered the same position with the Nebraska Republican Party. The Executive Director in Nebraska had called me asking for a recommendation, and I was thrilled for Olivia. I was also amused by the fact that the first question Olivia had asked during her interview process with Nebraska's GOP Chairman was, "You don't have a brother who is planning to run for Governor, do you?" She was assured he did not.

Almost immediately after my wife and I packed up and moved to Dayton, the Warner saga, after a couple of months' repose, took on a new life.

◆   ◆   ◆

In early April, West Virginia's State Senate Republican caucus, frustrated at a lack of support or activity from the State GOP, formally united to ask Kris to resign, and Hoppy Kercheval reported on his radio show that his own investigation indicated that GOP House members shared the same sentiment.

Then, WSAZ-TV reporter Scott Saxton reported on a memo he had discovered, a document apparently prepared by the former leader of the Mountaineer group just after the 2004 Primary, describing in detail the plans for the group's creation and implementation. Kris had always claimed the Mountaineer group was formed for the support of all candidates, but the most interesting part of the memo was its total focus on Monty Warner. This was a typical passage:

> *It was assumed that the outcome of the West Virginia Gubernatorial Primaries would be that Joe Manchin will win the Democrat Primary by 20% or more and Monty Warner would win the Republican Primary by a nose in a difficult horse race. This is exactly how it played out with Monty doing slightly better than expected. Expectations hereafter for Monty are very low—the vote for Joe Manchin in the Democrat primary was more than all votes cast in the Republican Primary. The game plan will therefore be to outperform those expectations. Since Monty will not likely win the fundraising battle, he must win at the grassroots level. The grassroots effort proposed here will make the difference for Monty to win on Election Day in November, 2004.*
>
> *Our plan for Monty is to create a communications network, both internally and externally, that can be understood perfectly by all, and is targeted specifically for: the general Electorate, the Republican and conservative Democrat base, our network of supporters, and our grassroots organization at every level. This is not just a short-term effort. It is designed to be the long-term framework for winning the campaign organizationally and politically, but also for governing.*

Kris again insisted to Saxton that the Mountaineer group was formed for the benefit of all candidates, not just Monty, but his denials meant little in light of this smoking gun. The calls for Kris to resign continued to grow, and the Secretary of State's office said it would investigate the document and the Mountaineer group.

Word also leaked that Kris was exploring the option of mortgaging GOP headquarters to pay off the debts, and that he had conducted a conference call with ten handpicked members of the State Executive Committee to gain approval for the move. I was curious as to whether Gayle Mason, a Committee member who had made it a personal mission over the previous two years to raise money to pay off our mortgage, had been included in the call. She said she had not. Kris eventually found out he could not legally take out a mortgage without the consent of the full Executive Committee.

◆   ◆   ◆

Later in April, the "Dump Warner" snowball started gathering serious steam. Delegate Craig Blair, whose fiery personality and bold approach often put him on the frontlines, unveiled a Web site he built called *MoveOnKris.org*. The site asked for Republicans to make pledges of money to pay off the Party debt, with the provision that Kris resign when the debt was erased. In less than a week, more money was pledged than the total amount of funds the Party itself had raised during the entire previous December, and about equal to the Party's month-by-month fundraising in the ensuing months.

The Internet was playing an increasingly important role in the Warner saga. A loose coalition of West Virginia Republicans seemed to seek each other out in the nether land of blogs, emails and Web sites. GOP consultant Mark Coyle (who had an email list of thousands of West Virginia grassroots activists and political reporters), former radio host Stephen Reed, former Young Republican Chair Charles Bolen, myself and others—many of whom had been at odds over the years—locked arms against our common foe. What's the old Arab proverb—the enemy of my enemy is my friend? Seldom was that truth more starkly evident. Together, this Internet Army shared the latest news, rumors, ideas and gossip with a growing and eager audience.

Additionally, a Huntington resident named Matt Pinson had long operated a well-read online news site, *huntingtonnews.net*, that routinely carried all the press releases issued by Charles Bolen, Craig Blair and others, as well as frequent, scathing Warner-bashing columns by "Sebastian Tutte," whose writing style was suspiciously similar to columns written over the years by Stephen Reed.

Then, surprising everyone, Hiram Lewis—Kris' handpicked Party Treasurer who had essentially blocked a vote on Kris in January with his parliamentary tactics—issued a press release calling on Kris to resign, adding to reporters that, hey, he might be interested in being Chairman himself. I was particularly amused by this one. I had long heard that Hiram had been critical of me for presenting Kris with the option of resigning and naming me interim Chairman back in November (Kris and Hiram had apparently found in my office the resignation letter I had prepared for Kris, in case he seemed willing to take that step). Hiram said that proposal was "high minded" of me.

Maybe it was, but now Hiram was doing exactly the same thing—the Party Treasurer calling on his Chairman to resign and offering himself as the alternative. The only difference I could see was that I had figured out Kris could no longer serve effectively about seven months before Hiram did. (Hiram abandoned the idea of becoming Chairman just a couple of days later.)

Nevertheless, both Blair's Web site and Lewis' press release got heavy media play throughout the state. Just a couple of days later, House of Delegates Minority Leader Charles Trump issued a press release calling for the State Executive Committee to replace Kris, followed by a letter signed by Trump, Senate Minority Leader Vic Sprouse, and new Secretary of State Betty Ireland, sent to all members of the State Executive Committee, again urging a change in leadership. In essence, that meant essentially that every Republican Legislator and statewide officeholder was on record calling on Kris to resign or be replaced.

The Ireland-Trump-Sprouse letter even went so far as to endorse the idea of Raleigh County Chairman Joe Long stepping in as interim Chairman. A couple of days later, Joe Long—who along with his wife, Julia, had done such a great job putting together our State Convention back in July—called me on my cell phone. After some small talk, he cut to the heart of the matter.

"Gary, are you ready to come back here and get back to work?" he asked.

I cautioned Joe about jumping the gun, and told him I did not expect Kris to give up the Chairmanship anytime soon, but Joe seemed to think otherwise. I wanted nothing more than to come back to the Party, but my personal circumstances had changed.

"Three months ago, I would have said 'absolutely,'" I told him. "Now, it's not so easy."

We talked a while longer, and I promised Joe I would help the Party any way I could, even if I could not return to work there full time.

The Associated Press' statehouse reporter, Larry Messina, wrote a story that appeared in most papers across the state on May 2. Messina wrote, "With a name like *MoveOnKris.org*, the site that popped up on the Internet last week was the latest, largest sign that West Virginia's Republican Party is in open revolt." The story recapped all the recent calls for Kris' resignation, and added, "The general election revealed the rift within the state GOP. Party members allege Warner squandered money and resources to aid the unsuccessful campaign of his brother, Monty Warner, the Republican nominee for governor. The rift grew more pronounced a few days after the election when Kris Warner fired Gary Abernathy, the party's popular executive director."

Whether I was "popular" or not was open for debate, but I knew such a description would not make Kris happy, which only bothered me in the context of whether it might further fortify his reluctance to resign.

Then, in early May, Kris suddenly announced a special meeting of the full State Executive Committee to be held May 21 in Morgantown to discuss "the future of the Party." For the first time, he allowed in a follow-up Associated Press story that he might consider resigning.

At the same time, another smoking gun was discovered, again thanks to the Internet—the online diary of a former member of the Mountaineer staff. Aside from describing the events from inside headquarters when Scott Saxton showed up with TV cameras on the day I was fired and the staff quit, the ex-Mountaineer had also detailed in previous entries the whole Mountaineer setup. I helped prepare a press release for former Young Republican Chairman Charles Bolen to issue on May 5.

It began, "A member of the notorious 'Mountaineer' group, aka Capitol Street gang, wrote that State Republican Party Chairman Kris Warner bought him a car, promised one employee a $10,000 'win bonus,' and 'is desperately throwing money around trying to rally support for the governor's race.'"

The release went on to reveal the details kept in the journal, including an instant message-style conversation between two Mountaineers describing how Kris had promised one of them $4500 a month plus the big "win bonus."

In another entry, from July 2004, the Mountaineer wrote, "The State Republican Party apparently raised $60,000 in back to back fundraisers this last week, and the chair is desperately throwing money around trying to rally support for the governor's race."

An August 24, 2004, entry read, "The car situation just got better. The state GOP Chair Kris Warner is buying me a $1000 car as part of a bonus because he knows I need it to be effective in the field. I can now make appointments and meet with my people without consequence. That's good, because I have nearly 2000 pages of precinct lists to deliver to them. I look forward to cruising around again...I did it all last summer and had a BLAST."

Bolen ended the press release by noting, "If there was any doubt left in anyone's mind what really happened during the 2004 campaign, this journal by a Mountaineer worker himself clears it up. I think just about all the questions about the party's debt and the Chairman's focus have now been answered."

The press release, thanks to Mark Coyle and others, got circulated to the email boxes of the media and, more importantly, members of the State Executive Committee. Within 48 hours, the entries in question had disappeared from the Web site—some panicky phone calls had obviously been made.

Then, on May 11, Hoppy Kercheval—no stranger to being the first to report important news—broke the story on his morning statewide radio show: Kris Warner was resigning. Or, so it seemed, anyway.

Hoppy read from a letter Kris had just issued to the State Executive Committee, but the content had Monty's style written all over it—its opening paragraph contained such identifiable and familiar strokes.

"Our amazing national progress may be traced to a divine development early in our history: a two-party political system," the letter began. "The pressing problems of the early Republic were seen to be best addressed by strong competing factions, who would bring forth all views, all information available, and all options for informed decisions."

When Monty gave a speech or preached to a captive audience, he could never resist offering his version of a history lesson and his notion of an appeal to patriotism. If he didn't write the letter, it at least exhibited evidence of his heavy influence.

"You are the concerned, civic-minded citizens of our day," the letter went on, addressing Committee members. "You are the Republican Party of West Virginia: the Party of Lincoln in the State created by Lincoln."

The two-page letter seemed to be trying almost painfully to get to a point, and finally listed six "cancers" currently eating away at the Republican Party, in the estimation of the letter writer, one of which, amazingly, "advances individuals at the expense of the Party and the State."

But almost hidden within the body of the letter was the statement, "I now ask you to let me resign my position as your Chairman and allow the Republican Revolution in this state to continue with a new leader."

Huh?

There is a way to resign. You simply say, "I hereby resign." But Kris Warner had to leave the door ajar if at all possible, with the somewhat ambiguous, "I now ask you to let me resign…"

I had to laugh to myself. Kris could now argue that he had resigned, sort of, but not really—not until and unless the Committee met at some unspecified date and "allowed" him to resign. Denying him the right to resign would result, apparently, in the Committee forcing Kris to serve as Chairman for life.

That evening, I called Bob Fish, who in addition to being the former leader of the ill-fated "Split Rail Committee" was also a Committee Vice Chairman, and reminded him that David Tyson had resigned in 2001 simply via the acceptance of the five Vice Chairs, who then turned around and appointed Kris Warner interim Chairman. Bob had already been thinking along those lines, and on Tuesday, May 11, 2005, that is what the Vice Chairs did, conferring via conference call and announcing it the next morning. Kris, quoted soon after in the *Gazette*, seemed to at last accept the finality of it.

"Warner said Wednesday that the vice chairpersons did exactly what they were supposed to do," wrote reporter Scott Finn. "He said he wishes the party well, but has no plans to be involved in it anymore." He also complained about the GOP going public with its inner-Party turmoil, saying the Democrats had the same problems, but kept them out of the press.

"The real difference is, the Republican Party has chosen to do it in a public matter. The Democrats do the same thing, but they keep it hidden," he said.

I shook my head at that one. Kris knew as well as anyone that Party members, including me and the staff, had gone to great lengths to keep the Party chaos out of the press as much as possible throughout the whole summer and Fall of 2004. Even after the election, he was offered a quiet and dignified exit. The whole sad episode only became a media soap opera after he ignored all overtures to deal quietly with the subject.

The simple fact remained that Kris Warner's chairmanship was effectively over the day he fired me and the staff walked out the door—not because we were so valuable or beloved, but because, on top of the Warner for Governor fiasco, it sent a message that never stopped ricocheting around the state. Losing your whole staff in such a public revolt signals a serious problem. Donors just refused to give, and money is indeed the lifeblood of politics. Without the ability to raise it, Kris was finished. The elected officials finally calling on Kris to resign had just sealed the deal.

For my part, I had to ask myself why I still cared, and why—having moved on to another city, another state, and another job—I was still helping where I could to bring an end to Kris Warner's reign. Was it pure vindictiveness on my part? Just an effort to get back at the individual who had fired me? Was I motivated only by revenge?

It would be foolish of me to pretend that wasn't part of it. Kris' firing of me had without doubt caused major problems in my life, both financial and emotional. But I have never been a vindictive person, and the idea of simply getting back at Kris Warner would not have sustained my involvement in subsequent events beyond a few days.

Yes, I had been paid to serve as Executive Director of the West Virginia Republican Party. But as is the case with many people, the job had become much more than a paycheck to me. Our target for success had become my baby as much as it had been Kris'—even more so, in my mind, since I believed Kris had abandoned the Party in favor of his brother's ambitions, while the rest of the staff and I had bought into the original vision and remained true to it. There was no amount of money in the world that made it worth Ben, Olivia, me or the rest of the headquarters' staff sticking with it during the last few months of the 2004 election. We rode it out because we cared.

As much as a part of me held onto the idea that I could return to the Party and help right the ship, I knew that wasn't going to happen. My wife was happy in Dayton, and wanted to stay. I had made a two-year commitment to my new employer, and I wasn't going back on it. So whether Kris officially resigned or not wouldn't mean anything to me in terms of my ability to return to the Party.

The sooner Kris left, though, the better chance the Party had of recapturing at least some of the momentum from the 2002 and 2004 elections, and what I had helped build could at least be somewhat salvaged, if not by me, then at least by some of the other capable Republicans in the state. And it wasn't my nature to walk away from a challenge. Kris had forced me out of the headquarters, but I could still help the Party keep moving forward, even if I had to do so from afar.

As for my feelings about Kris himself, I knew I would always have mixed emotions. Many people, including me, had warned him many times about the disaster that awaited the Party, and him personally, with his brother's gubernatorial campaign. Our worst fears were realized, and Kris even found more ways than we could imagine of alienating himself from Republicans, the media, his own staff, and many of his former friends. I can only guess what toll the entire sorry episode took on his own family. A part of me found it almost impossible to understand why there never came a point when he could see it before it was too late—if he ever saw it at all.

Sometimes, I think he knew what was coming all along. Just a few short days after my firing, I telephoned Kris on a matter unrelated to the Party. We both couldn't resist a small chuckle over the firestorm already brewing in the media—over my dismissal, the subsequent walk-out of the staff, the Bush-Warner signs, and the questions about the Party's involvement in the Warner for Governor campaign.

"Are you having fun yet?" I said with a quiet laugh.

"Never had more fun in my life," he said, equally amused.

It was the kind of humor to be found in such a situation only by the two people in the center of it—two people who knew each other all too well, and could almost read each other's mind.

During that brief conversation, the door was slightly opened by both of us for a possible reconciliation, and he suggested we talk again soon. But aside from a couple of brief phone calls when I was in Washington in January regarding tickets to the Presidential Inauguration for West Virginia's Republican delegation, we never spoke again.

Without a doubt, a part of me continued to have a fondness and a level of respect for Kris Warner, the friend with whom I traveled thousands of miles to seminars, conventions, late night candidate meetings and Lincoln Day Dinners. I missed the cohort with whom I had planned and schemed, celebrated victories, commiserated over losses, shared personal triumphs and travails.

There were many West Virginia Republicans who saw Kris as a villain. I never did. I saw him as a victim being pulled too many directions by too many personal and political demands. If I faulted him for anything, it was for failing to recognize the impossibility of accomplishing everything he took on—for not choosing between being Chairman of the Party, or Chief of Staff for his brother.

Like all of us, Kris Warner was a complicated combination of many lifelong influences, pressures, expectations, obligations and emotions. His love, loyalty and zeal for his brother had led him down a path during the 2004 campaign from which, politically, he could not return. My suggestion after the election that he resign—whether it was the right tactic for me to take or not—was not based on some desire to become Chairman myself. That was something that had never previously entered my mind. It was instead a sincere effort to keep our staff together, while sparing him from the events I knew would slowly unfold, with or without my involvement.

When it was all said and done, I wished him happiness, and I wished him peace.

Epilogue

There's nothing quite as unsatisfying as partial success. In three short years, the West Virginia Republican Party made impressive inroads in the formerly solid Democrat stronghold of West Virginia. We had accomplished a net pickup of 15 seats in the State Legislature. We twice reelected a Republican member of Congress, and helped President Bush carry the state by 13 points. We elected the first Republican Supreme Court Justice and Secretary of State in decades, and we grew Republican voter roles at a bigger rate than the Democrats.

And yet, what we failed to accomplish was a tragedy greater than the measure of our successes. When the dust settled from the 2004 elections, we should have been celebrating many more legislative wins. We should have been anticipating 2006 through the strength of a unified Party marching in lockstep toward the political takeover we had always predicted.

Instead, the story that emerged from the 2004 elections in West Virginia was that the State Party's victories and successes were far overshadowed by its self-inflicted injuries.

I'm proud of what we did accomplish in West Virginia. I'm proud of the best staff I've ever worked with, a staff comprised of bright and dedicated young politicos who struggled through several months of the most intense and debilitating pressure imaginable. Each one did what they could to help our legislative candidates, making the most of the meager tools left to us after we were drained of our funds and our enthusiasm.

But there are no experiences in life that are not beneficial in some way. My three years at the West Virginia Republican Party left me with many more positive experiences than negative ones. I met and married a wonderful West Virginia girl. I made countless new friends and important contacts in the political world, both inside and outside West Virginia, which I otherwise would not have made. I continued to learn new things—about politics, about life, about people.

Above all, I was reminded that blood is always thicker than water, and that the very best intentions are all too often destroyed by personal blind ambition. It's a lesson we all think we know, and yet somehow it happens time and time again.

978-0-595-35887-8
0-595-35887-X

www.ingramcontent.com/pod-product-compliance
Lightning Source LLC
Chambersburg PA
CBHW051409280526
45785CB00003B/1006